First World War
and Army of Occupation
War Diary
France, Belgium and Germany

39 DIVISION
116 Infantry Brigade
Royal Sussex Regiment
12th Battalion
4 March 1916 - 28 February 1918

WO95/2582/2

The Naval & Military Press Ltd
www.nmarchive.com
Published in association with The National Archives

Published by

The Naval & Military Press Ltd

Unit 10 Ridgewood Industrial Park,

Uckfield, East Sussex,

TN22 5QE England

Tel: +44 (0) 1825 749494

www.naval-military-press.com

www.nmarchive.com

This diary has been reprinted in facsimile from the original. Any imperfections are inevitably reproduced and the quality may fall short of modern type and cartographic standards.

© **Crown Copyright**
Images reproduced by permission of The National Archives, London, England, 2015.

Contents

Document type	Place/Title	Date From	Date To
Heading	12th Battalion Royal Sussex Regiment		
Heading	39th Division 116 Bde 12 Bn R Sussex Regt 1916 Mar-1918 Feb Disbanded.		
Heading	116th Brigade 39th Division France 12th Battalion Royal Sussex Regt. Jan-Feb 1918		
Heading	116th Brigade 39th Division. Battalion Disembarked Havre 5.3.16 12th Battalion The Royal Sussex Regiment March 1916		
Heading	War Diary of 12th Bn Royal Sussex Regt From 4th Mar 1916 To 31st Mar 1916		
War Diary	Witley Camp.	04/03/1916	04/03/1916
War Diary	Havre	05/03/1916	05/03/1916
War Diary	Sandvic	06/03/1916	06/03/1916
War Diary	Morbecque	07/03/1916	11/03/1916
War Diary	Estaires	12/03/1916	12/03/1916
War Diary	Fleurbaix	12/03/1916	23/03/1916
War Diary	Estaires	24/03/1916	26/03/1916
War Diary	Lagorgue	27/03/1916	31/03/1916
Heading	116th Brigade. 39th Division. 12th Battalion The Royal Sussex Regiment April 1916		
War Diary	Lagorgue	01/04/1916	01/04/1916
War Diary	Caudescure	14/04/1916	14/04/1916
War Diary	Riez Du Vinage	15/04/1916	15/04/1916
War Diary	Windy Corner	19/04/1916	19/04/1916
War Diary	Givenchy	23/04/1916	23/04/1916
War Diary	Gorre	27/04/1916	27/04/1916
War Diary	Caudescure	14/04/1916	14/04/1916
War Diary	Gorre	27/04/1916	30/04/1916
Heading	116th Brigade. 39th Division. 12th Battalion The Royal Sussex Regiment May 1916		
War Diary	Givenchy	01/05/1916	01/05/1916
War Diary	Les Choquax	09/05/1916	09/05/1916
War Diary	Festubert	13/05/1916	17/05/1916
War Diary	Le Touret	21/05/1916	21/05/1916
War Diary	Festubert	25/05/1916	25/05/1916
War Diary	Les Choquax	28/05/1916	28/05/1916
Heading	116th Brigade. 39th Division. 12th Battalion The Royal Sussex Regiment June 1916		
War Diary	Annaquin North	01/06/1916	01/06/1916
War Diary	Cuinchy	05/06/1916	10/06/1916
War Diary	Le Quesnay	11/06/1916	11/06/1916
War Diary	Les. Choquaux	16/06/1916	16/06/1916
War Diary	Ferme Du Bois	21/06/1916	21/06/1916
War Diary	Croix Barbee	22/06/1916	22/06/1916
War Diary	Les Lobes	28/06/1916	28/06/1916
War Diary	Ferme Du Bois	29/06/1916	30/06/1916
Miscellaneous	Officers' Casualties During Engagement Of 30th June, 1916	30/06/1916	30/06/1916
Operation(al) Order(s)	Operation Order No. 20	26/06/1916	26/06/1916

Heading	116th Brigade. 39th Division. 12th Battalion The Royal Sussex Regiment July 1916		
Heading	War Diary of 12th Bn. R. Sussex R. From 1st July 1916 To 31st July 1916		
War Diary	Les Lobes	03/07/1916	06/07/1916
War Diary	Bethune	07/07/1916	07/07/1916
War Diary	Annequin S.	08/07/1916	08/07/1916
War Diary	Village Line Cuinchy.	10/07/1916	10/07/1916
War Diary	Cuinchy	11/07/1916	11/07/1916
War Diary	Cuinchy Left Subsector (1)	12/07/1916	13/07/1916
War Diary	Annequin. S.	14/07/1916	16/07/1916
War Diary	Le Hamel	20/07/1916	20/07/1916
War Diary	Ferme Du Bois (Report Sector)	24/07/1916	24/07/1916
War Diary	Festubert Line.	24/07/1916	28/07/1916
War Diary	Festubert Right Sector.	31/07/1916	31/07/1916
Heading	116th Brigade. 39th Division. 12th Battalion The Royal Sussex Regiment August 1916		
Miscellaneous	12th Bn R Sussex Regt	07/09/1916	07/09/1916
War Diary	Festubert R.S.E	01/08/1916	02/08/1916
War Diary	Le Hamel	02/08/1916	06/08/1916
War Diary	Gwenchy Les La Basse.	07/08/1916	07/08/1916
War Diary	Gwenchy	08/08/1916	11/08/1916
War Diary	Auchel	13/08/1916	22/08/1916
War Diary	Monchy Breton	23/08/1916	23/08/1916
War Diary	Sibiville	24/08/1916	24/08/1916
War Diary	Sus St Leger	25/08/1916	25/08/1916
War Diary	Bois Du Warnemont	26/08/1916	27/08/1916
War Diary	Near Englebelmer	28/08/1916	31/08/1916
Heading	116th Brigade. 39th Division. 12th Battalion The Royal Sussex Regiment September 1916		
Miscellaneous	Headquarters 116 Infantry Brigade	01/10/1916	01/10/1916
War Diary	Near Englebelmer	01/09/1916	02/09/1916
War Diary	Mesnil	03/09/1916	03/09/1916
War Diary	Fort Moulin	04/09/1916	04/09/1916
War Diary	Near Englebelmer	05/09/1916	10/09/1916
War Diary	Auchonvillers	11/09/1916	14/09/1916
War Diary	Beaussart	15/09/1916	19/09/1916
War Diary	Redan	20/09/1916	29/09/1916
War Diary	Mailly-Maillet	30/09/1916	30/09/1916
Heading	116th Brigade. 39th Division.12th Battalion The Royal Sussex Regiment October 1916		
Heading	War Diary of 12th Bn. Royal Sussex Regt For The Month Of Oct 1916		
War Diary	Mailly-Maillet	01/10/1916	03/10/1916
War Diary	Auchonvillers	03/10/1916	06/10/1916
War Diary	White City	07/10/1916	14/10/1916
War Diary	Schwaben Redoubt	15/10/1916	17/10/1916
War Diary	Aveluy	18/10/1916	20/10/1916
War Diary	Schwaben Redoubt	21/10/1916	22/10/1916
War Diary	Martinsart	23/10/1916	25/11/1916
War Diary	Pioneer Rd	26/11/1916	27/11/1916
War Diary	N. Bluff Authville	29/10/1916	30/10/1916
Heading	116th Brigade. 39th Division. 12th Battalion The Royal Sussex Regiment November 1916		
Heading	War Diary of 12th Bn Royal Sussex Regt. Nov 1st 1916 To Nov 30th 1916 Vol IX		

War Diary	N. Bluff Authville	01/11/1916	03/11/1916
War Diary	Senlis	03/11/1916	05/11/1916
War Diary	Martinsart	06/11/1916	08/11/1916
War Diary	Paisley Dump	09/11/1916	13/11/1916
War Diary	Warloy	14/11/1916	14/11/1916
War Diary	Doullens	15/11/1916	17/11/1916
War Diary	Poperinghe	18/11/1916	30/11/1916
Heading	116th Brigade. 39th Division. 12th Battalion The Royal Sussex Regiment December 1916		
Heading	War Diary For 12th Bn Royal Sussex Regt. For December 1916 Vol 10		
War Diary	N. Camp Poperinghe.	01/12/1916	10/12/1916
War Diary	Canal Bank	11/12/1916	20/12/1916
War Diary	Irish Farm	21/12/1916	24/12/1916
War Diary	D Camp Nr. Poperinghe	24/12/1916	29/12/1916
War Diary	Machine Gun Farm	30/12/1916	31/12/1916
Heading	12th Bn Royal Sussex Regt War Diary For The Month Of January 1917 Vol XI.		
War Diary	Machine Gun Farm	01/01/1917	15/01/1917
War Diary	Ry Wood Rt Subsec	16/01/1917	20/01/1917
War Diary	Ypres	21/01/1917	24/01/1917
War Diary	Railway Wood Section	24/01/1917	31/01/1917
War Diary	Vaux-Sur-Somme	30/01/1918	30/01/1918
War Diary	Haut Allaines (Nr. Peronne)	31/01/1918	31/01/1918
Heading	War Diary For The Month Of February 1917 12th Bn R. Sussex Regt Vol XII		
War Diary	Railway Wood	01/02/1917	14/02/1917
War Diary	Millain	15/02/1917	23/02/1917
War Diary	Montreal Camp.	24/02/1917	24/02/1917
War Diary	Zillebeke Bund	25/02/1917	27/02/1917
War Diary	Rudkin Ho.	28/02/1917	28/02/1917
Heading	War Diary of 12th Bn. Royal Sussex R. For March 1917 Vol 13		
War Diary	Rudkin Ho.	01/03/1917	03/03/1917
War Diary	Montreal Camp	04/03/1917	09/03/1917
War Diary	Kruistaart	10/03/1917	13/03/1917
War Diary	Rudkin Ho.	13/03/1917	17/03/1917
War Diary	Zillebeke Bund	17/03/1917	22/03/1917
War Diary	Montreal Camp	22/03/1917	26/03/1917
War Diary	Rudkin Ho.	27/03/1917	31/03/1917
Heading	War Diary of 12th Bn R. Sussex Regt. For April 1917 Vol 14		
War Diary	Kruisstraat	01/04/1917	04/04/1917
War Diary	Rudkin House	05/04/1917	07/04/1917
War Diary	Brandhoek	07/04/1917	11/04/1917
War Diary	Tuilieries	11/04/1917	16/04/1917
War Diary	Brandhoek	16/04/1917	16/04/1917
War Diary	Irish Farm	17/04/1917	23/04/1917
War Diary	Canal Bank	24/04/1917	29/04/1917
War Diary	Z Camp	29/04/1917	30/04/1917
Miscellaneous	Headquarters, 116th. Infantry Brigade.	01/06/1917	01/06/1917
War Diary	Z Camp	30/04/1917	30/04/1917
War Diary	Wizernes	01/05/1917	01/05/1917
War Diary	Acquin	02/05/1917	11/05/1917
War Diary	Wizernes	14/05/1917	14/05/1917
War Diary	Oehtezeele	15/05/1917	15/05/1917

War Diary	Wormhoult	16/05/1917	28/05/1917
War Diary	Ypres	28/05/1917	28/05/1917
War Diary	O Camp.	29/05/1917	31/05/1917
War Diary	Hilltop	01/06/1917	05/06/1917
War Diary	Canal Bank	06/06/1917	09/06/1917
War Diary	Hilltop Rd Subsector.	10/06/1917	15/06/1917
War Diary	O. Camp	16/06/1917	20/06/1917
War Diary	Moule	21/06/1917	17/07/1917
War Diary	O. Camp.	18/07/1917	28/07/1917
War Diary	Hill Top	29/07/1917	31/07/1917
War Diary	Mouse Trap Farm	01/08/1917	02/08/1917
War Diary	Canal Bank	03/08/1917	03/08/1917
War Diary	K. Camp	04/08/1917	07/08/1917
War Diary	Meterum.	08/08/1917	12/08/1917
War Diary	Ridgewood Camp.	12/08/1917	13/08/1917
War Diary	Hollebeke	14/08/1917	18/08/1917
War Diary	Bois Confluent	18/08/1917	20/08/1917
War Diary	Hollebeke	21/08/1917	23/08/1917
War Diary	Ridgewood Camp.	24/08/1917	27/08/1917
War Diary	Klein Zillebeke	28/08/1917	31/08/1917
War Diary	Ridge. Wood	02/09/1917	02/09/1917
War Diary	Chippewa	04/09/1917	04/09/1917
War Diary	Voormezeele	08/09/1917	08/09/1917
War Diary	Zwartleen	09/09/1917	09/09/1917
War Diary	Ridgewood	12/09/1917	12/09/1917
War Diary	Zwartleen	15/09/1917	16/09/1917
War Diary	Westoutre Kempton Park	18/09/1917	20/09/1917
War Diary	Beggars Rest.	22/09/1917	22/09/1917
War Diary	Tower Hamlets	23/09/1917	27/09/1917
War Diary	Near Berthen Shi 27.R23. 4.7	28/09/1917	28/09/1917
War Diary	Ref: Kokereele	28/09/1917	14/10/1917
War Diary	Tower Hamlets.	15/10/1917	18/10/1917
War Diary	Canada Street	18/10/1917	20/10/1917
War Diary	Willebeek N.9.d.7.5	21/10/1917	22/10/1917
War Diary	Willebeek	23/10/1917	23/10/1917
War Diary	Dezon Annexe	24/10/1917	28/10/1917
War Diary	Morrumbidgee	29/10/1917	03/11/1917
War Diary	Tower Hamlets	06/11/1917	07/11/1917
War Diary	Morrumbidgee	08/11/1917	09/11/1917
War Diary	Tower Hamlets	13/11/1917	16/11/1917
War Diary	Hedge St	20/11/1917	20/11/1917
War Diary	Tower Hamlets	21/11/1917	24/11/1917
War Diary	Hedge St.	26/11/1917	26/11/1917
War Diary	Chippewa Camp	27/11/1917	27/11/1917
War Diary		28/11/1917	30/11/1917
War Diary	Poperinghe	01/12/1917	07/12/1917
War Diary	Winnizeele	10/12/1917	10/12/1917
War Diary	Seninghem	13/12/1917	28/12/1917
War Diary	Lottinghem	29/12/1917	29/12/1917
War Diary	Seninghem	30/12/1917	30/12/1917
War Diary	Hospital. Farm	31/12/1917	31/12/1917
Miscellaneous	Headquarters. 116th Inf. Brigade.	31/01/1918	31/01/1918
War Diary	Hospital Farm	01/01/1918	06/01/1918
War Diary	Irish Fm Camp	07/01/1918	15/01/1918
War Diary	Corps Line	16/01/1918	16/01/1918
War Diary	Steenbeek Defences	17/01/1918	18/01/1918

War Diary	Westroosebeke (Rf. Front)	18/01/1918	21/01/1918
War Diary	Schools Camp.	22/01/1918	22/01/1918
War Diary	Poperinghe	23/01/1918	26/01/1918
War Diary	Vaux-Sur-Somme	27/01/1918	29/01/1918
War Diary	Haut Allaines (Nr. Peronne)	01/02/1918	01/02/1918
War Diary	Gauche-Wood Sub. Sector	04/02/1918	04/02/1918
War Diary	Heudecourt	05/02/1918	14/02/1918
War Diary	Haut Allaines	16/02/1918	16/02/1918
War Diary	Sorel	17/02/1918	17/02/1918
War Diary	Hamel	18/02/1918	20/02/1918
War Diary	Haut Allaines	22/02/1918	28/02/1918

12TH BATTALION ROYAL SUSSEX REGIMENT

39 DIVISION

116 BDE

12 BN R SUSSEX REGT

1916 MAR — 1918 FEB

DISBANDED

116TH BRIGADE
39TH DIVISION

FRANCE
12TH BATTALION
ROYAL SUSSEX REGT.
JAN - FEB 1918

116th Brigade
39th Division.
444444444444

BATTALION DISEMBARKED HAVRE 5.3.16.

12th BATTALION

THE ROYAL SUSSEX REGIMENT

MARCH 1 9 1 6

12 Sussex
Vol 2
116/39
XXXIV

Army Form C. 2118.

G.D. I.F.
Sohm

WAR DIARY
or
INTELLIGENCE SUMMARY.
(Erase heading not required.)

Instructions regarding War Diaries and Intelligence Summaries are contained in F. S. Regs., Part II. and the Staff Manual respectively. Title pages will be prepared in manuscript.

— Confidential —

War Diary
of
12th Bn. Royal Sussex Regt

from 4th Mar. 1916
Do 31st Mar. 1916

Place	Date	Hour	Summary of Events and Information	Remarks and references to Appendices

T2134. Wt. W708—776. 500000. 4/15. Sir J. C. & S.

Army Form C. 2118.

WAR DIARY
or
INTELLIGENCE SUMMARY.
(Erase heading not required.)

Instructions regarding War Diaries and Intelligence Summaries are contained in F. S. Regs, Part II and the Staff Manual respectively. Title pages will be prepared in manuscript.

Place	Date	Hour	Summary of Events and Information	Remarks and references to Appendices
WITLEY CAMP	4.3.16		Batt. proceeded by rail to SOUTHAMPTON. Embarked for HAVRE.	
HAVRE	5.3.16		Arrived 2 am. Disembarked 7 am. Marched to rest camp for night	
SAN DYIG	6.3.16		Batt. entrained for MORBECQUE.	
MORBECQUE	7.3.16		Arrived 1 p.m. Debarked. Marched to Camp.	
"	8.3.16		Remained in Camp.	
"	9.3.16		" " "	
"	10.3.16		" " "	
"	11.3.16		" " "	
ESTAIRES	12.3.16	4am	Batt. marched to ESTAIRES. Billeted for the night	
"	"	4.30 pm	Right half Bn. marched to FLEURBAIX. There attached to 8th Bn. K.O.Y.L.I. for instruction	
FLEURBAIX	"	9 pm	Left " " " " " " 11th Sherwood Foresters	
"	13.3.16		Right half Bn. went into trenches for instruction	
"	"		Left " " " " " "	
"	"		Remained in billets. Found working fatigue parties	
"	14.3.16		Right half Bn. in trenches. Left half Bn. in billets which were shelled	
"	15.3.16		Left half Bn. relieved right half Bn. in trenches for instruction	
"	16.3.16		Left half Bn. in trenches. Right half Bn. in billets, found working fatigue parties	

Army Form C. 2118.

WAR DIARY
INTELLIGENCE SUMMARY

(Erase heading not required.)

Instructions regarding War Diaries and Intelligence Summaries are contained in F. S. Regs., Part II. and the Staff Manual respectively. Title pages will be prepared in manuscript.

Place	Date	Hour	Summary of Events and Information	Remarks and references to Appendices
FLEURBAIX	17.3.16		Left half Bn in trenches, right half Bn in billets, found working parties for fatigues.	
"	18.3.16		Right half Bn relieves left half Bn in trenches.	
"	19.3.16		Left half Bn in billets, found fatigues & working parties. Right half in trenches.	
"	20.3.16		Whole Bn took over the line.	
"	21.3.16		Battalion in trenches.	
"	22.3.16		"	
"	23.3.16 9pm		Battalion relieved by 10th Bn Lincoln Regt. marched to billets at ESTAIRES.	
ESTAIRES	24.3.16 1am		Whole Bn went into billets.	
"	25.3.16		remained in billets	
"	26.3.16 10pm		marched to LA GORGUE & went into billets.	
LA GORGUE	27.3.16		remained in billets	
"	28.3.16		"	
"	29.3.16		"	
"	30.3.16		"	
"	31.3.16 1.0pm		Bn marched to MERVILLE & went into billets at LE LAURIER	

116th Brigade.
39th Division.

12th BATTALION

THE ROYAL SUSSEX REGIMENT

APRIL 1916

WAR DIARY
INTELLIGENCE SUMMARY
(Erase heading not required)

Army Form C. 2118.

Place	Date	Hour	Summary of Events and Information	Remarks and references to Appendices
LACOUTURE	14.4.16		Bn marched to CAUDESCURE and the MERVILLE pleasant so billets 14.4.16	CAUDESCURE Divisional Reserve
CAUDESCURE	19.4.16		Bn marched to RIEZ DU VINAGE pleasant village in billets	16/4/16 7 OR wounded 1 OR wounded 1 OR killed
RIEZ DU VINAGE	15.4.16		" marched to WINDY CORNER, relief the GIVENCHY sect. relieved Welsh Regt	19/4/1
WINDY CORNER	19.4.16		Bn relieved 14th Hauck in front line GIVENCHY	In Trenches 7 OR wounded
GIVENCHY	23.4.16		" moved back to huts in GORRE	20/4/16 7 OR wounded 2 OR wounded
GORRE	27.4.16		" relieved 13th Hauck in front line & relieved here 30.4.16	22/4/ 2 OR wounded 6 OR wounded
CAUDESCURE	14.4.16		Brig. Genl. Graham CB gave us Summary of the Brigade	27/4/16 1 OR wounded
GORRE	27.4.16		Lt Col Walker gave up Command of the Battn	28/4/16 1 OR killed 1 OR wounded
	30.4.		Lt Col Impey Assumed Command of Battn.	29/4/16 THREE wounded

116th Brigade.
39th Division

12th BATTALION

THE ROYAL SUSSEX REGIMENT

M A Y 1 9 1 6

Copy of — 12th Bn Royal Sussex Regt

Army Form C. 2118

WAR DIARY
INTELLIGENCE SUMMARY
(Erase heading not required.)

XXX'X or Vol 3

May 1916

S.F.
1 sheet

Place	Date	Hour	Summary of Events and Information	Remarks and references to Appendices
GIVENCHY	1-5-16		Bn. marched back to billets in LES CHOQUAX	Casualties during month
Les CHOQUAX	9-5-16		Bn. relieved 12th Rifle Brigade in village line FESTUBERT	4/5/16 1.O.R. killed
FESTUBERT	13-5-16		Bn. moved up into O.B.L. & Islands	2 O.R. wounded 1/5/16
"	17-5-16		Bn. marched back to billets in LE TOURET	3 O.R wounded 4/5/16
LE TOURET	21-5-16		Bn. moved into front line (O.B.L. & Islands) FESTUBERT	1 Officer wounded 4/5/16
FESTUBERT	25-5-16		Bn. marched back to billets at LES CHOQUAX	2 O.R. killed 4/5/16 1 O.R. wounded
LES CHOQUAX	28-5-16		Bn relieved 1st Middlesex Regt in ANNEQUIN NORTH	7/5/16 2.O.R. killed 1.O.R. wounded 4/5/16 1.O.R. wounded 29/5/16 1.O.R. wounded 29/5/16 1.O.R. wounded

116th Brigade.
39th Division.

12th BATTALION

THE ROYAL SUSSEX REGIMENT

JUNE 1916

WAR DIARY or INTELLIGENCE SUMMARY

Army Form C. 2118.

12th Bn Reg Berks Regt
vol 4

June 1916

Place	Date	Hour	Summary of Events and Information	Remarks and references to Appendices
ANNEQUIN NORTH	1.6.16		Relieved 14th Hants in front line CUINCHY	
CUINCHY	5.6.16		Bn moved back to village line. Relieved by 14th Hants	
"	8.6.16		" into front line CUINCHY, relieved 14th Hants	
"	16.6.16		" relieved by 14th Middlesex, moved back to billets at LES CHOQUAUX QUESNAY	
LE QUESNAY	11.6.16		" moved back to base Pl'age to billets at LES CHOQUAUX	
LES CHOQUAUX	18.6.16		" relieved 3rd Cheshire Regt in front line at FERME DU BOIS (Spontini)	
FERME DU BOIS	20.6.16		" moved back to CROIX BARBÉE	
CROIX BARBÉE	22.6.16		" moved to LES LOBES in Divn Reserve	
LES LOBES	28.6.16		" moved to RICHEBOURG	

Army Form C. 2118

WAR DIARY
or
INTELLIGENCE SUMMARY
(Erase heading not required.)

1st (O) Battⁿ
R. Sussex Regt

Instructions regarding War Diaries and Intelligence Summaries are contained in F.S. Regs., Part II. and the Staff Manual respectively. Title Pages will be prepared in manuscript.

Place	Date	Hour	Summary of Events and Information	Remarks and references to Appendices
LES LOBES	28/6/16	8pm	Two Companies marched to front line trenches opp sector FERME DU BOIS	Casualties 30/6/16
			RICHBOURG	O.R.
			VIELLE CHAPELLE	(Killed) 21
FERME DU BOIS	29/6/16	9pm	Two Companies relieved front line FERME DU BOIS, RICHBOURG & VIELLE CHAPELLE opposite trenches hundred enemy trenches BOARS HEAD from 9pm to 6.5pm	missing 35 wounded 236
			Artillery bombarded enemy trenches BOARS HEAD from 9pm to 6.5pm	known 120
—	30/6/16	3.5am	Battalion attacked enemy front support line & succeeded in about 3 hours the front line & had the withdrawal ordered by the supply of bombs & ammunition being cut off by enemy artillery barrage on our front line commenced trenches, preventing reinforcements being sent forward.	Nos 412
			Our men relieved attacked & strong counter attacks were silenced by the gt strength to 20 men marched attached The Battalion was relieved by the gt strength to 20 men marched attached to LES LOBES after resting at RICHBOURG.	

Officers' Casualties during engagement of
30th June, 1916.

Lt. Col. Impey, G. H.	Wounded
Captain Cotton, A. N.	Killed in action
Lieut. Boys, S. C.	Wounded
" Sparks, C.	Killed in action.
" Robinson, H. C. T.	Wounded
2/Lieut. Fenchelle, G. J.	Killed in action
" Ambler, G.	Wounded
" Arkcoll, F. T.	Killed in action
" Hanby, F. J.	Missing
" Moody, L. L.	Killed in action
" Mercer, J.	Wounded
" Dorman, C. C. B.	Wounded
" Moyle, F. W.	Missing
" Ardill, J.	Missing
" Swallow, S. H.	Missing
" Mason, F. A.	Wounded
" Salberg. J. B.	Missing

26th June, 1916.   SECRET

OPERATION ORDER   No. 20
----

1. **Intention**   To capture the enemy's trenches between the BOARS
   HEAD and the salient about S.10.c.9.5., viz :-
   Enemy front line from BOARS HEAD to S.10.c.9.5.
   Enemy support line from S.16.a.5½.6½. to S.10.d 1.3.

2. **Frontage**   The frontage allotted to the 12th Bn. is from Ditch
   from our front line S.10.c.5.3. to S.10.c.8.0., i.e.:-
   the frontage between the junction of XXXXXX HAZARA &
   VINE STREET with our present front line.

   The 13th Bn. are allotted the right section of the assault.

3. **Composition**   The Battalion will assault in 4 lines of platoons,
   of   "A" Coy. with its right on the ditch about 30 yards N.
   Assaulting   of VINE STREET, "B", "C" & "D" Coys. with its left in
   Columns   HAZARA STREET; each Coy. to have approximately 20 yards
   of frontage.

   The columns will be dispersed as follows :-
   1st Wave
                    4 Assaulting Platoons

   "D" Coy. - 1 Assaulting Platoon.
              2 special bombing & blocking parties for
                 blocks 7 & 6 and support trenches leading
                 up to them.
              1 Coy. Bombing Squad to bomb up communication
                 trench between D & C points.

   "C" Coy.   1 Assaulting Platoon.
              1 Coy. Bombing Squad for 7 communication
                 trench and trenches of support line to
                 left to join up with "D" Coy.

   "B" Coy.   1 Assaulting Platoon.
              1 special bombing & blocking party to bomb
                 up Z communication trench to block S.
              1 Coy. bombing squad to bomb along support
                 line & join up with "C" Coy.

   "A" Coy.   1 Assaulting Platoon.
              2 special bombing & blocking squads to deal
                 with communication trench to blocks 4 & 3.
              2 Coy. bombing squads to bomb along the two
                 support trenches towards Z trench.

   2nd Wave
              4 Assaulting Platoons.
              A reserve Coy. bombing squad will be told
                 off from each Platoon.

   3rd Wave
              4 Assaulting Platoons.

   "D" Coy.   1 special bombing & blocking party to deal
                 with front line to block 8.
              Each platoon will detail 1 bombing squad to
                 clear the enemy's front line as follows :-
                 Each squad to work from its right to left
                 flank until it joins up with the Coy. on its
                 left.

   4th Wave
              4 Assaulting Platoons.
              Each platoon to detail one reserve bombing
                 squad.

(2)

    <u>Lewis Guns</u> The 4 Lewis Guns will accompany the last wave and will join their Companies as occasion requires.

    <u>Snipers</u> (1) Six pairs will be selected by each of the Assaulting Battalions, in conjunction with the Brigade Sniping Officer.

    (2) These snipers will advance with the third wave of their respective Battalions, and on their outer flanks.

    (3) On arrival in the new trenches they will take up suitable posts for sniping and observation.

    (4) When all the Battalion Snipers have taken up their posts, the Battalion Sniping N.C.O. will send a report to his Bn. Hdqrs., from which it will be sent on to the Brigade Sniping Officer at VINE STREET H.Q.

4. <u>Assembly of Column</u> Nos. 1 & 2 waves, plus the specialist parties, will assemble in the front line trench between HAZARA STREET and VINE STREET.

Nos. 3 & 4 Waves will similarly assemble in the support line between these 2 points.

The definite allotment of frontage of each platoon will be decided upon on the ground.

5. <u>The Assault</u> At a.m. on the the Artillery will lift and the Assault will be carried by waves as detailed in para. 3.

The 1st Wave will immediately go over the parapet & will be followed by the second, 3rd & 4th Waves, as soon as possible.

The platoons will be formed in lines, and with their specialists parties immediately in rear of them and on the flank nearest to their allotted task.

The objective of the 1st & 2nd Waves is the enemy's support trenches, and the platoons concerned will on no account stop at the enemy's front line.

The objective of the 3rd & 4th Waves will be the enemy's front line.

O.C.Coys. will ascertain assure that certain men of the Coy. bombing squads are told off to deal with dug-outs.

6. <u>Consolidation</u> The work of consolidating the new trenches will be undertaken at once.

Special typed instructions have been issued to each Company Commander on the subject.

The R.E. are constructing strong points at A,B,B2,C & D, as per attached sketch.

The 116th Bde. M G. Coy will supply Vickers Guns for these strong points.

7. <u>STORES</u>

<u>Ammunition</u> Two extra bandoliers will be issued to each man, which, with the 120 rounds already carried, will make 220 rounds per rifle.

There will be a close reserve of 100 rounds per rifle at the following points :-

A Coy. VINE STREET (Northern Side)..... 15 boxes
B Coy. COPSE STREET (do.)..... 15 boxes
C Coy. COPSE STREET (do.)..... 15 boxes
D Coy. HAZARA STREET (do.)..... 15 boxes

A Brigade Reserve of 50 rounds per rifle will be stored at the junction of GUARDS and VINE STREET.

8. <u>Bombs</u> Bomb Stores will be established under Brigade arrangements as follows :-

<u>First Reserve Store</u>
A Coy. at forward end of VINE ST. (Southern side)..500
B & C Coys. " " "COPSE ST. (do.)1,600
D Coy. = = =HAZARA ST. (do.)..800

(3)

  Second Reserve Store
   Junction HAZARA STREET and GUARDS.................. 6,000

  Third Reserve Store (Brigade Reserve)
   At junction of VINE STREET with GUARDS trench....... 6,000

8. **R.E.Stores** Dumps for R.E.Stores will be at the head of COPSE STREET and HAZARA STREET.

9. **Rations & Water** Each man will carry 1 days rations & a full waterbottle.
  Water will be stored in petrol cans etc. at convenient points against the front line parapet.
  Stores for rations and water will be established as follows :-
   A Coy. at forward end of VINE STREET
   B Coy. " " " " COPSE STREET
   C Coy. " " " " COPSE STREET
   D Coy. " " " " HAZARA STREET

10. **Stores** Within our New Lines
  Within our new lines, Ammunition, Stores, Bomb Stores, Dumps for R.E.Stores and Tools, and Stores for Rations and Water will at once be constructed and filled up as detailed above.

11. **Equipment** Marching Order No. 2, i.e. without packs.
  Each man to carry his waterproof sheet on back of his belt.
  Arrangements regarding the dumping of packs & great coats will be notified later.
  All ranks will carry 2 bombs. These will on no account be used except by order of an Officer. They will be collected, if possible, under instructions of Platoon Commanders, to form a reserve.

  Tools and Sandbags will be carried as follows :-

	Picks & Shovels	Sandbags
First Wave...........	-	1 per man
Second Wave..........	Each man 1 tool	2 " "
Third Wave...........	Each man 1 tool	4 " "
Fourth Wave..........	Each man 1 tool	4 " "

12. **Carrying Parties** A carrying party of 20 men has been detailed from the H.Q Staff, Pioneers, etc.
  O.C.Coys. will detail a further 6 men.
  Lieut.C.O.Bolton will be in charge of the R.E Stores, Rations & Water.
  2/Lieut.H.T.K.Robinson will be in charge of the bomb & S.A.A.Stores, and will be responsible for the supply of same to front line.
  These Officers will arrange together the distribution of the carrying parties. O.C.Coys. will detail one reliable N C.O. to assist these Officers.

13. **Communication** See Appendix 1.

14. **Special Warning** The order "RETIRE" will not be given, and should this particular word be heard it must be understood that it emanates from no one in authority.

15. **Runners** O.C.Coys. will ensure that all Runners make themselves well acquainted with the various H.Q. & Signal Stations.

16. **Medical Arrangements** All wounded will be evacuated via HAZARA STREET and tramway.

17. **Battalion H.Q's** Battalion H.Q's will be at a point in COPSE STREET half way between that trench and GUARDS.

     (sd) G. H. IMPEY, Lieut. Colonel.
       Commanding, L. B. B.

116th Brigade.
39th Division.

12th BATTALION

THE ROYAL SUSSEX REGIMENT

JULY 1916

89/vol 5

Confidential

War Diary

of

12th Div. A Plumer R.

from 1st July 1916 to 31st July 1916

July 1916

1st (S) Batt. Royal Sussex R.

WAR DIARY
INTELLIGENCE SUMMARY
(Erase heading not required.)

Army Form C. 2118.

Place	Date	Hour	Summary of Events and Information	Remarks and references to Appendices
LES LOGES	3/7/16		Battalion inspected by Divisional and Corps Commanders	Cavalier
—	5/7/16		Two officers taken on strength of Battn. Capt. J. Moolan 2nd Lt. J.C. Yates	
—	6/7/16	10 pm	Battalion marched to BETHUNE. Billets École de Jeunes filles	10/7/16 2nd Lt. Tremlett
BETHUNE	7/7/16	8.45 pm	Battalion to ANNEQUIN. S. took over billets from 2nd Royal Fusiliers	
ANNEQUIN S. VILLAGE LINE CUINCHY	8/7/16	10 pm	Battn. occupied trenches VILLAGE LINE CUINCHY	12/7/16 10 R Yates 2nd Lt. Tremlett
CUINCHY	10/7/16		Battalion relieved 12th Gloucesters in KEEPS CUINCHY area	
	11/7/16	10 pm	Battalion moved to front line trenches occupying Sections 20 to 26 in left subsection O relieving two companies 14th Hants. 8 officers taken on strength of Battalion: 2nd Lieuts. Come Taylor, Strickland, 7BR Kenno, Wm. Racey, Geo. Ivy, L. Morgan, E. Dawson, Strickland.	
CUINCHY Left Subsect. O	13/7/16	10.30 pm	Battalion stood to for 3 hours owing to information being received from S.O.C. 118th Inf. Bde. that enemy would begin trench to trench be ...	
			Casualties from enemy bombardment	
—	14/7/16	8 pm	Battalion wire had to put. Killed ANNEQUIN S. Brig. photo by 14th Hants. 5 officers taken on strength of Battalion Capt. Zybalur, Lieut Rd. Barrett 2nd Lt. W. Bailey LCC 2nd Lt. G.B. Ritchie, 2nd Lt. Elliott RH	
ANNEQUIN S.	15/7/16			

Army Form C. 2118.

WAR DIARY
or
INTELLIGENCE SUMMARY.
(Erase heading not required.)

July 1916
1st/1st Batt
Royal Sussex Regt

Place	Date	Hour	Summary of Events and Information	Remarks and references to Appendices
ANNEQUIN S.	26/7/16	1 a.m.	Battalion marched into billets at LE HAMEL	Appendices
LE HAMEL	28/7/16		Battalion amalgamated with 13th R Sussex Regt marched to FERME DU BOIS	28/7/16 1078 rank + file
			Right sector relieving 5th Notts Derby	
FERME DU BOIS (Right Sector)	29/7/16	10 a.m.	Battalion left tindle occupied billets FESTUBERT village line + livery in company at Le Tombe at LE PLANTIN	29/7/16 10 R recently killed
FESTUBERT Village Line	29/7/16		Draft of 197 NCO's & men arrived. 8 Officers taken on strength of Battalion. Lt A Helm & 2nd Lt H.R. Randall Lt Arnold L.A. Andrews L Seymour 2nd Lt Stephens, Mr Hill, S.R. Fulcher, Lt Dove	29/7/16 1 OR killed 2 OR wounded
	29/7/16	4 pm	Battalion relieved 14th Hants in 073 L & Island FESTUBERT Right	31/7/16 3 OR wounded
FESTUBERT Right Sector	31/7/16		Enemy shelled 10RANDS 10.70a during in considerable amount of damage but causing no slight casualties	

R Quincey Major
O C 1/12 Rt Sussex Regt

116th Brigade.
39th Division½.

12th BATTALION

THE ROYAL SUSSEX REGIMENT

AUGUST 1 9 1 6

12th Bn R Sussex Regt
7-9-1916.

Officer i/c New Army, Infantry Sec No 5
Base.

War Diary for month
of August herewith

> A.G's
> OFFICE AT THE BASE.
> No.
> Date
> REGULAR INFANTRY
> SECTION No. 5.

for Lt & Adjt
C.C.

A.A.A.G (I)
Passed to you please
12/9/16   i/c No 5 Reg. Army Inf Sect.

Army Form C. 2118

39 — 12. R. Scots — Vol 6

WAR DIARY
or
INTELLIGENCE SUMMARY
(Erase heading not required.)

Instructions regarding War Diaries and Intelligence Summaries are contained in F. S. Regs., Part II. and the Staff Manual respectively. Title Pages will be prepared in manuscript.

Place	Date	Hour	Summary of Events and Information	Remarks and references to Appendices
Hs Robert R.53.	1.8.16.		Day quiet. Relieved by 4/5 Black Watch. Battalion proceeds to billets in LE HAMEL. All in billets by	
LE HAMEL	2.8.16 / 5.8.16		Training in billets at LE HAMEL. Musketry, Route marching and Gas Chamber. Weather continuously fine & hot.	
"	6.8.16.		Capt. Cassey takes over command of the Battalion from Major Bellamy D.S.O. who has taken part in the great Commemorative Church Parade service at 140 turn Bethune when General Sir Charles Munro 1st Army makes his last public appearance in France. Battalion proceeds to Givenchy section. Takes over village line from 16th R.B. 117 Inf. (Gr) Relief complete 11.30 p.m. 23rd Bde. on our right, 118th Bde. on our left.	
Givenchy lez la Bassée	7.8.16.		Very quiet day throughout. Enemy shelling Cotheme with very large calibre gun, probably 15". Nothing further to report.	

Army Form C. 2118

WAR DIARY
or
INTELLIGENCE SUMMARY
(Erase heading not required.)

Instructions regarding War Diaries and Intelligence Summaries are contained in F. S. Regs., Part II. and the Staff Manual respectively. Title Pages will be prepared in manuscript.

Place	Date	Hour	Summary of Events and Information	Remarks and references to Appendices
Givenchy	8.8.16 – 10.8.16		Nothing of Importance to report. Weather good. Village line Quiet.	
	11.8.16	6.a.m.	Relieved by 2nd Yorkshire Regt. a march to FERME DU ROI (near Bethune). Dinners eaten there.	
		6 p.m.	The Battalion proceeded to billets at AUCHEL. All in billets at 11.30 p.m.	
Auchel	13.8.16	6.15 am	Battalion marched to Bois du Ligne. Dinners & tea eaten there.	
		5.30 pm	Battalion proceeded to billets at Monchy Breton. All in billets at 8.45 pm.	
	14.8.16 – 21.8.16		Training carried on under Brigade arrangements, on the 17th Army training area.	
	21.8.16		Capt. J. M. Finlay takes over command of Battalion during the absence of Capt Barry (each) temporary	
	22.8.16		Training continued under Brigade arrangements	

Army Form C. 2118

WAR DIARY
or
INTELLIGENCE SUMMARY
(Erase heading not required.)

Instructions regarding War Diaries and Intelligence Summaries are contained in F. S. Regs., Part II. and the Staff Manual respectively. Title Pages will be prepared in manuscript.

Place	Date	Hour	Summary of Events and Information	Remarks and references to Appendices
Monchy Breton	23/8/16		Battalion proceeds to Dubrulle and takes over billets at 11-30 a.m.	
Sibiville	24/8/16		Battalion proceeds to billets at Dus St Leger and takes over at 10 a.m.	
Dus St Leger	25/8/16		Battalion marched to camp in Bois du Warnimont arrived at 2 p.m.	
Bois du Warnimont	26/8/16		Battalion rested after 3 days successive marching	
do	27/8/16		Weather Bad. Battalion left camp in evening and marched to bivouacs near Englebelmer arrived about 9-30 p.m.	
New Englebelmer	28/8/16 29/8/16		Weather continued Bad. Large working parties found by Battalion on 28 & 29th. Reconnoitring front line in front of HAMEL & new support positions & communications	

1875   Wt. W593/826 1,000,000 4/15 J.B.C. & A. A.D.S.S./Forms/C. 2118.

Army Form C. 2118

WAR DIARY
or
INTELLIGENCE SUMMARY

(Erase heading not required.)

Instructions regarding War Diaries and Intelligence Summaries are contained in F.S. Regs., Part II. and the Staff Manual respectively. Title Pages will be prepared in manuscript.

Place	Date	Hour	Summary of Events and Information	Remarks and references to Appendices
Near Englebelmer	30/8/16		Carried out by 10 Officers. N.C.O's & selected men	
do	31/8/16		Remained in bivouacs. Woods in close proximity heavily shelled by enemy both by day and night	
do	1/9/16		Moved to fresh bivouacs owing to continued enemy shelling.	
do	2/9/16		Quiet day, remained in bivouacs. Weather fine	

116th Brigade.
39th Divison.

12th BATTALION

THE ROYAL SUSSEX REGIMENT

SEPTEMBER 1 9 1 6

12th Bn R Suss R.
1-10-1916

Headquarters
116 Infantry Brigade

War diary for month
of September herewith

[signature]

Lieut & afadjt
for O.C.

Army Form C. 2118

12 B Sussex

Vol 7

T.O

T.F
J Smith

WAR DIARY
INTELLIGENCE SUMMARY
(Erase heading not required.)

Place	Date	Hour	Summary of Events and Information	Remarks and references to Appendices
Near Englebelmer	1/7/16		Quiet day remained in bivouacs	
"	2/7/16		Weather fine. Whole Battalion detailed for carrying & working parties in connection with attack on following day. Headquarters of Battalion moved to MESNIL in the evening; all parties joined units to which they were attached.	
MESNIL	3/7/16	5-10 a.m.	The 39th Division attacked enemy's position immediately N. River ANCRE. Objective – enemy's third line. Objective reached but found impossible to hold. Portion of enemy's front line held until 6 p.m. troops then withdrawn. Battalion re-assembled in HAMEL, relieved at 7 p.m. by 1/16th Cheshires, & proceeded to FORT MOULIN. Casualties in Battalion :- 1 Officer 1 killed, 2 missing + 3 wounded	

1875 Wt. W593/826 1,000,000 4/15 J.B.C. & A. A.D.S.S./Forms/C. 2118.

WAR DIARY or INTELLIGENCE SUMMARY

(Erase heading not required.)

Army Form C. 2118

Place	Date	Hour	Summary of Events and Information	Remarks and references to Appendices
Fort Moulin	4/9/16		Other Ranks Killed 5, Wounded 54, Missing 20. Remained here for day, returned to Bivouacs previously occupied near Engelbelmer in evening	
near Engelbelmer	5/9/16		Weather bad. Enemy shelled neighbourhood of Bivouacs. Draft of 100 other ranks arrived in evening	
do	6/9/16		Battalion rested in bivouacs. Enemy shelled neighbourhood during night	
do	7/9/16		Training commenced under regimental arrangements. Capt. A.C. Allen takes over temporary command of Battalion vice Capt. J.M. Henley - sick to hospital.	
do	8/9/16		Training - all specialists separately - remainder of Battalion entrenching. Draft of 48 arrived in evening.	

WAR DIARY

INTELLIGENCE SUMMARY

(Erase heading not required.)

Army Form C. 2118

Instructions regarding War Diaries and Intelligence Summaries are contained in F. S. Regs., Part II. and the Staff Manual respectively. Title Pages will be prepared in manuscript.

Place	Date	Hour	Summary of Events and Information	Remarks and references to Appendices
Near Englebelmer	9/6		Training continued. Reconnaissance of AUCHONVILLERS Right sub-sector carried out by Officers & N.C.O's	
	10/6		Battalion took over from 4th Royal Berks in front line in AUCHONVILLERS. Relief complete 11-15 a.m. Enemy fairly active during night	Casualties 3. O.R wounded
Auchonvillers	11/6		Fairly quiet day. Auchonvillers shelled during day with 4.2 & 5.9 shrapnel. Wiring of front line commenced. Support line shelled during evening	Casualties 3. O.R wounded
do	12/6		Considerable progress made with wiring of, and with deepening of communication trench joining our front line with left Battalion. Draft of 160 O.R arrived	
do	13/6		Deepening of communication trench completed. Great progress made with clearing up and repairing	

WAR DIARY
INTELLIGENCE SUMMARY
(Erase heading not required.)

Army Form C. 2118

Instructions regarding War Diaries and Intelligence Summaries are contained in F.S. Regs., Part II. and the Staff Manual respectively. Title Pages will be prepared in manuscript.

Place	Date	Hour	Summary of Events and Information	Remarks and references to Appendices
	14/10		trenches. Intermittent enemy shelling throughout the day and night	
Beaussart	15/10		Battalion relieved by 11th Bn. R. Innis. R. Relief complete 12.20 p.m. Battalion moved back to billets at BEAUSSART. Billeting complete 2 p.m.	
do	16/10		Battalion training in Brigade reserve. Baths at ACHEUX and BERTRANCOURT used by Battalion. Bept of heavy rgmed and took over command. Training continued. Particular attention being paid to specialists. Lt Col. J.W. Impey rejoined from England and reassumed command of Battalion.	
do	17/10		Battalion rested. Church Parade - trenches - Surcease to Huplain.	
do	18/10		Weather very bad all day. Reconnaissance of	

WAR DIARY
INTELLIGENCE SUMMARY

(Erase heading not required.)

Army Form C. 2118

Place	Date	Hour	Summary of Events and Information	Remarks and references to Appendices
Arras	19/9/16	7 p.m.	To REDAN left sub-section carried by 2 coy commanding Officers, Officers & N.C.O's. Battalion left billets & marched to trenches.	
REDAN	20/9/16		Getting used to new Coy. + Bdes. O.C. Brig. Regt. Left billets REDAN Battalion HdQrs. being heavily shelled at intervals during day Battalion HdQrs. again heavily shelled during day nearly right. Trenches in bad condition owing to rain	
"	21/9/16 to 25/9/16		Considerable progress made clearing and repairing trenches, casualties much improved being used during two reliefs	25/9/16 Another 2 O.R. wound
"	26/9/16	12.35 p.m.	The 39 Div. North launched a final attack at 0.0.20 & K.35.a.22 in conjunction with the real attack on our right. The artillery and trench mortars seem to have been for him, the arrangements for smoke bomb & hummers has to be carried away to improvise and being sufficient to give impression of attack.	10 O.R. killed 6 O.R. wounded
"	27/9/16 to 30/9/16		Every thing has been calm on this front. Considerable improvement effected in condition of trenches.	

WAR DIARY or INTELLIGENCE SUMMARY

Army Form C. 2118

Place	Date	Hour	Summary of Events and Information	Remarks and references to Appendices
MAILLY-MAILLET	30/9/16	8pm	Battalion was relieved in the REDAN sector by the 2nd Batln Royal Fusiliers marched into billets at MAILLY MAILLET Corps Reserve.	1 OR wounded

D Vaughan Capt.
for O.C. 1st Rifle Brigade

116th Brigade.
39th Division.

12th BATTALION

THE ROYAL SUSSEX REGIMENT

OCTOBER 1 9 1 6

Confidential
116/39

War Diary
of
12th B. Royal Sussex Regt
for the month of
Oct. 1916

Army Form C. 2118

WAR DIARY
or
INTELLIGENCE SUMMARY
(Erase heading not required.)

Place	Date	Hour	Summary of Events and Information	Remarks and references to Appendices
Mailly-Maillet	1/10/16 to 2/10/16		Battn. in Brigade Reserve at Mailly-Maillet, and employed each night in carrying parties Trench Mortar bombs up to gun emplacements in line in Auchonvillers South Sector.	
Auchonvillers	3/10/16		Battn. moved to Auchonvillers in Brigade Reserve, relieving the 2nd y. n.E. Royal Sussex Regt.	
	3/10/16 to 5/10/16		Battn. still employed carrying munition T.M. Bombs.	
"	6/10/16		Two Companies (B & D) moved to bivouacs in Englebelmer woods.	
White City	7/10/16		Battn. relieved 14th Bn Hampshire Regt. in Auchonvillers North Sector. Relief complete by 5 P.M. Front extending from Junction of Watling St & Clive French to Beaumont Hamel Road. Quiet night.	5 O.R. wounded
"	8/10/16		Battn: front extended South to Broadway. Thirty relieving on an 2. 13th R. Sussex Regt: relief complete by 10 P.M. Our artillery active during day - enemy wire & front support trenches - enemy reply feeble.	3 O.R. killed 2 O.R. wounded
"	9/10/16 to 11/10/16		Our artillery & T.Ms active in wire cutting & bombardment of enemy line. Enemy retaliated to some extent with T.Ms & 77 mm shells. Our trenches slightly damaged, but repaired each night. Enemy appear to have few heavy guns opposite us in this sector.	4 O.R. killed 5 O.R. wounded

Army Form C. 2118.

WAR DIARY
or
INTELLIGENCE SUMMARY.
(Erase heading not required.)

Instructions regarding War Diaries and Intelligence Summaries are contained in F.S. Regs., Part II. and the Staff Manual respectively. Title pages will be prepared in manuscript.

Place	Date	Hour	Summary of Events and Information	Remarks and references to Appendices
White City	12/10/16 to 14/10/16	—	Generally quiet. Our artillery shelled enemy support and reserve lines and disposed working party to North of Beaumont Hamel. On the night 12/13 October enemy blew up in front of Hunter Trench in two places with heavy T.Ms.	S.O.R. shells 4. H.O.R. wounded
"	14/10/13		Battalion relieved by 13th R. Sussex Regt. by 11 P.M and proceeded to bivouac in Engelbelmer Wood.	
Schwaben Redoubt	15/10/16		Battⁿ paraded at 3 A.M. and marched to hutments in Pioneer Rd. near Martinsart. At 4.30 P.M. Battⁿ headed marched to relieve detachments of 118th Infy Brigade in Schwaben Redoubt. Owing to darkness & guides losing their way relief was not complete until 5 A.M 16/10/16. Relief was carried into under a heavy barrage causing us a good many casualties. About 10 P.M. enemy attacked D Coy on left of Schwaben Redoubt coming up Strasburg Trench & using flammenwerfers. This attack was completely beaten off with heavy loss to the enemy.	1 Officer killed 1 Officer missing 3 Officers wounded 4. O.R. killed 85. O.R. wounded 51. O.R. missing from 15th to 17th

T2134. Wt. W708—776. 500000. 4/15. Sir J.C.&S.

Army Form C. 2118.

WAR DIARY
or
INTELLIGENCE SUMMARY.
(Erase heading not required.)

Instructions regarding War Diaries and Intelligence Summaries are contained in F. S. Regs., Part II. and the Staff Manual respectively. Title pages will be prepared in manuscript.

Place	Date	Hour	Summary of Events and Information	Remarks and references to Appendices
Schwaben Redoubt	16/10/16		Enemy made small bombing attack which was easily beaten off in early hours of morning. Day quiet except for intermittent shelling.	
	17/10/16		Another small bombing attack which was repulsed. At 3 p.m. enemy commenced a heavy bombardment of the redoubt with 5.9 & 8 inch shells, which lasted until 8.30 p.m. Our artillery replied vigorously. During the bombardment the Battn was relieved by 14th Hampshire Regiment. Relief complete by 9 p.m., and Battn proceeded to billets at Aveluy. Casualties 5 Officers 156 O.R.	
Aveluy	18/10/16		Battn in billets at Aveluy.	
	19/10/16		Still at Aveluy. A Coy relieved a Coy of the 14th Hampshire Regt in support line of Schwaben Redoubt.	
	20/10/16		Battn still at Aveluy. A Coy relieved by a Coy of 17th K.R. Rifles & returned to Aveluy at 11.30 P.M.	
Schwaben Redoubt	21/10/16		Battn marched to Wood Post taking over from 13th R. Sussex R. at 10 P.M. At 10.15 A.M. C Coy marched to Schwaben Redoubt to support in attack with other units of 116th Inft. Brigade on later part in attack with other units of 116th Inft Brigade on	21/10 - 22/10 6 B.O.R. wounded 26 O.R. missing

T2134. Wt. W708—776. 500000. 4/15. Sir J. C. & S.

Army Form C. 2118.

WAR DIARY
or
INTELLIGENCE SUMMARY.
(Erase heading not required.)

Instructions regarding War Diaries and Intelligence Summaries are contained in F.S. Regs., Part II. and the Staff Manual respectively. Title pages will be prepared in manuscript.

Place	Date	Hour	Summary of Events and Information	Remarks and references to Appendices
Schwaben Redoubt	21/10/16		Stuff Trench, which was completely successful. Battⁿ marched at 4.30 P.M. to relieve detachments of 14th H. to 17th K.R. Rifles in Stuff Trench & Schwaben Redoubt.	
	22/10/16		Night quiet, spent in digging in new front line trench. Battⁿ relieved by 7th S. Lancs R. Relief complete by 7 P.M. br. carried out under a heavy barrage. Casualties during attack and relief 2 Offrs, 60 O.R. Battⁿ proceeded to hutments nr Martinsart. Battⁿ in hutments at Martinsart. Time spent in refitting	
Martinsart	23/10/16 24/10/16		the Battⁿ in necessary equipment.	
	25/10/16		Battⁿ relieved 17th Notts Derby Regt in centre sector of River section	
Pioneer Rd.	26/10/16		On the whole quiet, time spent in cleaning trenches, dugouts, bringing dud. 5 O.R. wounded	5 O.R. wounded
	27/10/16		Relieved by 17th Notts & Derby Regt & Battⁿ proceeded to huts in Pioneer	
N. Bluff	28/10/16 29/10/16		Road, remained there until 30 October 1916.	3 O.R. wounded
Authville	30/10/16		Battⁿ relieved 4/5th Black Watch in centre sector of River section	
			Ops were heavily shelled from 6 to 7.30 P.M.	
	31/10/16		Generally quiet, except that C of R cpl were killed from 6 to 7.30 P.M.	3 O.R. killed 6 O.R. wounded

H.T.R. Ortmann
for O.C. 12 R. Scots R. Captᵗ 31/11/16

116th Brigade.
39th Division.

12th BATTALION

THE ROYAL SUSSEX REGIMENT

NOVEMBER 1 9 1 6

Vol 9

War Diary
of
12th Bn Royal Sussex Regt

November 1st 1916 to October 30th 96

Vol IX

9.F.

WAR DIARY
or
INTELLIGENCE SUMMARY.
(Erase heading not required.)

Army Form C. 2118.

Place	Date	Hour	Summary of Events and Information	Remarks and references to Appendices
N. Bluff Authuile	1/11/16 to		Batt'n were relieved by 1/1st Herts Reg't. Relief Complete by 2.30 P.M. Batt'n went into Bgde onto at N.Bluff, Authuile, & remained there two days.	1. O.R. Killed 8.O.R wounded
	3/11/16			
Senlis	3/11/16		Batt'n moved to Senlis under canvas.	
	4/11/16		Large working party furnished to unload trucks at Aveluy. Batt'n moved up into Bgde Reserve at Thiepval. The	
	5/11/16		Batt'n were occupied during early hours of the night in making a road through Trenches Crucifix Corner	2 O.R wounded
Martinsart	6/11/16		Batt'n were relieved by 16 Rifle Brigade and proceeded to huts in Martinsart Wood.	
	7/11/16		Batt'n remained in huts at Martinsart Wood.	
	8/11/16		do.	
Authuile Dump	9/11/16		Batt'n relieved 1/1st Herts in left Sector of River Sector - Relief Complete by 2.30 p.m.	
"	10/11/16 to 15/11/16		Time spent in improving front line along Brick Road and in joining up with Central sector of River Sector	

WAR DIARY
or
INTELLIGENCE SUMMARY.
(Erase heading not required.)

Army Form C. 2118.

Place	Date	Hour	Summary of Events and Information	Remarks and references to Appendices
Priez Dump	13/9/16		Division attacked S. Pierre Divion & Hansa line at noon extensively successful many prisoners captured and casualties light. The 12th Royal Sussex were in reserve & moved to take part in the attack but were not called upon to take part in it. Battn moved in the evening to North Bluff, Authuille.	
Warloy	14/9/16		Battn marched to billets at Warloy.	
Domleux	15/9/16		Battn marched to billets in Domleux	
"	16/9/16		Battn rested in billets at Domleux	
"	17/9/16		Battn entraining for Longpré.	
Offranges	18/9/16		Battn went into "K" lines near Offranges.	
"	19-22		Coy, Platoon & Company training in trenches.	
"	23/9/16		Inspection by G.O.C. VIIIth Corps.	
"	24-26		Coy training in trenches	
"	27/9/16		Route march & manoeuvre.	
"	28/9/16			
"	30/9/16		Battn. steadily training in trenches	

T2134. Wt. W708-776. 500000. 4/15. Sir J. C. & S.

116th Brigade.
39th Division.

12th BATTALION

THE ROYAL SUSSEX REGIMENT

DECEMBER 1 9 1 6

Confidential

Vol 10

War Diary
for
12th Dr. Royal Sussex Regt
December 1916

Vol 10

10.F.
5 sheet

WAR DIARY
INTELLIGENCE SUMMARY
(Erase heading not required.)

Army Form C. 2118.

Place	Date	Hour	Summary of Events and Information	Remarks and references to Appendices
K Camp Poperinghe	1/12/16		Training in camp - improvements made to trenches	
"	2/12/16		do. Final Company football match played "C" Coy top of league	
"	3/12/16		Church Parade, rest, recreation	
"	4/12/16		Battn. Route March. Gas helmet practice	
"	5/12/16		Shooting on miniature range & gas helmet practice	
"	6/12/16		Brigade Route March. Inspection by G.O.C. 2nd Army	
"	7/12/16		Shooting on miniature range & other training	
"	8/12/16		do.	
"	9/12/16		General training in accordance with programme. General idea night	
"	10/12/16		Church Parade, rest, recreation	
"	11/12/16		Marched to Poperinghe, entrained to Ypres and relieved 10th S.W.B. in Canal Bank	
Canal Bank	12/12/16		Relieved 11th S. & 13th in Riflex sector & Hill 60 top Section. Relief complete 9 p.m.	Casualties
"	13/12/16		Quiet day. 24 hrs spent in digging, training, repairing parapet etc	1. O.R wounded
"	14/12/16		Slight shelling on right Coy front	1. O.R killed 1 Officer wounded
"	15/12/16		Enemy patrol's active during night	1. O.R wounded
"	16/12/16		Relieved by 14th Hampshire Regt. Relief complete by 7.30 P.M.	

WAR DIARY
or
INTELLIGENCE SUMMARY.

(Erase heading not required.)

Army Form C. 2118.

Place	Date	Hour	Summary of Events and Information	Remarks and references to Appendices
Canal Bank	17/12/16 to 20/12/16		Battn. in support on Canal Bank. Time spent in training, and work. Working parties being furnished every night and to support lines during the day. Battn. relieved 14th Hampshire Regt. in right Subsector of Hilltop sector. Relief complete by 7.50 p.m.	
Irish Farm	21/12/16 to 24/12/16		Quiet considerable artillery activity on right. Slight retaliation by enemy on Bilge Trench. Little damage done. Enemy patrols more active on night of 23/24 December. On patrol encountered one of the enemy and a fight ensued. We had four casualties. Enemy casualties unknown.	Casualties 4. O.R. wounded
D Camp Poperinghe	24/12/16		Relieved by 4/5th Royal Highlanders. Relief complete by 8.30 p.m. Marched back to D Camp arriving there before midnight.	
"	25/12/16 26/12/16		Battn. held Xmas dinner. Day spent in usual recreation. Day spent in cleaning up equipment. Camp.	
"	27/12/16 to 29/12/16		Time spent in training. Musketry, bayonet fighting, arms drill, with a route march on 29th instant. An excellent concert	

WAR DIARY
or
INTELLIGENCE SUMMARY
(Erase heading not required.)

Army Form C. 2118.

Place	Date	Hour	Summary of Events and Information	Remarks and references to Appendices
D Camp W (Reninghelst)			was held in the Church Army hut in the evening of the 28th instant. Improvements to camp. Tarred felt has been used to stop up whole Battn. latrines improved and properly covered floors & huts mended.	
Machine Gun Coy 31st Div Farm	29/11/17		Relieved 16th Welsh Regt in "L" Line Broodseinde Sector. Relief complete by 7 P.M. Day spent in working - improvements made in defences of posts	

JJR Roberts
Major
1/2 R. Sussex Regt
1 Decr 1917.

A.H. 11.F.
4 sheet

Confidential

12th Bn. Royal Sussex Regt. Vol XI

War Diary
for
the month of January 1919

Vol XI

WAR DIARY or INTELLIGENCE SUMMARY

Army Form C. 2118.

Place	Date	Hour	Summary of Events and Information	Remarks and references to Appendices
Finedone Gurdon	1/1/17 to 14/1/17		Batt. in ELVERDINGHE. References to line. Time spent in Training. Saluting, arms drill, gas helmet drills etc. Much improvement in defences. Batts. were working under R.E. supervision, greatly improving strong points in L1, L2, L3, L4, L5, L6 . Various improvements in interior economy were made in the area on positions notably new field oven this were incinerators in L4 for men, new field oven in L4 — Batt. also a day we were released in L4. One releasement in L4 + a new one constructed. On the evening of the 13th January 1917 the Batt. relieved 1/4th Batt. Loyal North Lancs Regt. in Ypres.	
Ry Wood Welsulse	16/1/17		Battalion relieved 1/4 Loyal North Lancs in right sub section.	
	18/1/17		Intercompany relief B.C. relieved A.D in front line	Casualties
	20/1/17		On the night 20/21 Bn was relieved by 13/N Sussex after uneventful tour, two companies proceeded to Earls Manor Lk + 2 to the Ramparts in Ypres	20.0 Wounded

WAR DIARY
INTELLIGENCE SUMMARY

Army Form C. 2118.

Place	Date	Hour	Summary of Events and Information	Remarks and references to Appendices
Ypres	23/1/17		Working parties of 3 Officers & 60 men per day & 5 Officers & 200 men per night found nightly for work on defences.	
	24/1/17			
Railway field Sector	24/1/17		At night 24th Bn relieved the 13th Bn Ross Regt in right sub sector. At 5:30am at morning of 25th the enemy opened heavy bombardment on our left Co & on M Co of left Bn (11th Rileman) the S.O.S. was put up but the enemy did not attempt to enter our trenches. At 5:45 the artillery activity died down.	Casualties 1. O.R. killed 3. O.R. wounded
	25/1/17		Gas alarm was given about 7pm. Believed to come from left Battalion. This was found to be false.	
	26/1/17		S.O.S. was seen to go up some distance on our left but no developments took place.	
	27/1/17		Lancer birthday but nothing unusual occurred.	
	28/1/17		Battalion relieved by 13th Rifleman returned to Eagle Chen comp-- were in Ramparts	
	29/1/17		Heard working parties furnished few shells in Salve.	
	30/1/17			
	31/1/17		Nothing of importance	

P. Very Kerr
Lt. Col.
R.C.R. Irish Regt
1st Feb 1917

Army Form C. 2118.

WAR DIARY
or
INTELLIGENCE SUMMARY.
(Erase heading not required.)

Instructions regarding War Diaries and Intelligence Summaries are contained in F. S. Regs., Part II. and the Staff Manual respectively. Title pages will be prepared in manuscript.

Place	Date	Hour	Summary of Events and Information	Remarks and references to Appendices
VAUX-BAR-SONNE	30/4/18	5 am	New Camp near PERONNE. Battalion marched to COPPIE and entrained for PERONNE.	
"			Proceeded to Camp at HAUT ALLAINES. All in Camp 2 pm	
HAUT ALLAINES (N. PERONNE)	31/4/18		Battalion in Divisional Reserve. Rested in camp. Weather very cold. Usual advance parties proceeded to front line to take over from 6' KOSB in right sub sector of Centre Sector.	

W. Cooke-Brown Lt Col.
R.S.F. Commanding

(A7833) Wt. W89/M1672 350,000 4/17 D. D. & L., London, E.C. Sch. 52a. Forms/C/2118/4

Confidential

Vol 12

War Diary

for

the month of February 1914

2nd Bn R. Sussex Regt

Vol XII

12.F.
Habut

Army Form C. 2118.

WAR DIARY
or
INTELLIGENCE SUMMARY.
(Erase heading not required.)

Instructions regarding War Diaries and Intelligence Summaries are contained in F. S. Regs., Part II. and the Staff Manual respectively. Title pages will be prepared in manuscript.

Place	Date	Hour	Summary of Events and Information	Remarks and references to Appendices
Anbury Wood	1/2/17		Relieved 13 Pl. Sirens in evening in Right Sector N Subsection	
	2/2/17		Nothing of importance	
	3/2/17		At 1am 10 am the enemy blew in mine on the Pl. companys front. He occupied the crater & consolidated it. No hostile attack or bombardment followed. Relieved at night by 17th Sherwood Foresters, proceeded to Eala leaving C coy support line	Casualties killed 2 officers & 6 O.R. Wounded 4 O.R. Missing 7 O.R.
	4/2/17		Relieved in Eala support line by 17 KRR	
	5/2/17			
	14/2/17		In B Camp Manual training carried on	
	15/2/17		Entrained at Cheesemarket Station Poperinghe for Battn Bollezeele, and marched to MILLAIN, being relieved in B Camp by 1/5th Kings Liverpools	
Millain	16/2/17		In MILLAIN - usual training carried on with recreation in the afternoon	
	23/2/17	}	Staffs Sports. Supervised at BOLLEZEELE to POPERINGHE and marched to MONTREAL CAMP BRANDHOEK, and their entrained at 7.30 p.m. for	
	24/2/17			
	25/2/17			
Montreal Camp Zillebeke Brood			ASYLUM STATION, YPRES - Relieved the 10th WEST RIDING REGT. in support in the OBSERVATORY & Sector Relief complete 1.45 A.M	
	26/2/17		Battalion engaged in carrying on working parties for front line	

Army Form C. 2118.

WAR DIARY
or
INTELLIGENCE SUMMARY.
(Erase heading not required.)

Instructions regarding War Diaries and Intelligence Summaries are contained in F. S. Regs., Part II. and the Staff Manual respectively. Title pages will be prepared in manuscript.

Place	Date	Hour	Summary of Events and Information	Remarks and references to Appendices
ZILLEBE	27/4/17		Batt'n employed in carrying and on working parties for front line	
BUND RUDKIN H.Q.	28/4/17		Relieved 13th Royal Sussex Reg't in right sub sector of OBSERVATORY WOOD sector. Relief complete by	

L.B. 18.F.
5 sheet

Confidential vol 13

War Diary
of
Lt. Br. Royal Sussex R.
Jr
March 1917.

WAR DIARY
or
INTELLIGENCE SUMMARY.
(Erase heading not required.)

Army Form C. 2118.

Place	Date	Hour	Summary of Events and Information	Remarks and references to Appendices
~~Montreal~~ Rudkin No 1	1/3/17		On the night 28 Feb - 1 March, enemy bombarded our front line & support line heavily with artillery & trench mortars, and attempted the about Kla about to make an attack - enemy however the effective reply of our artillery & machine gun fire was frustrated. S. Peter's St., J. Dundon St. were badly damaged.	3 O.R. killed 22 O.R. wounded
	2/3/17		Quiet day. Slight artillery activity by enemy.	3 O.R. killed
	3/3/17		Relieved by 1/5th Cheshire Regiment. Relief complete by 11.30 P.M. Marched to Y/PRES ASYLUM STN & entrained K.B.R. & J.H.O.E.R. marching from there to MONTREAL CAMP.	
MONTREAL CAMP	4/3/17 to 5		Usual training carried out - the camp was inspected by the Corps Commander on 5 March, and a concert held in the evening to celebrate the anniversary of the landing of the Division in France.	
	9/3/17		Relieved 1/1st Cambridgeshire Regt. in Divisional Reserve in the OBSERVATORY RIDGE sector. Relief complete by 7.45 p.m.	
	10/3/17 to 13/3/17		Batt'n in Divisional reserve, engaged in working parties in front line & in front of support lines.	
KRUISTAART	13/3/17		Relieved 13. F. Batt'n Royal Sussex Regt in right subsector 2 nicht	
RUDKIN NO				

Army Form C. 2118.

WAR DIARY
or
INTELLIGENCE SUMMARY.
(Erase heading not required.)

Instructions regarding War Diaries and Intelligence Summaries are contained in F. S. Regs., Part II. and the Staff Manual respectively. Title pages will be prepared in manuscript.

Place	Date	Hour	Summary of Events and Information	Remarks and references to Appendices
RUDKIN HR.	13/3/17		Sector of OBSERVATORY RIDGE. Relief complete by 11.30 p.m.	Casualties
	14/3/17 to 17/3/17		Batt'n in the line. Considerable work done in wiring in front of the front line & close support trenches. except for desultory shelling Enemy very quiet.	2 OR. killed 4 OR. wounded
ZILLEBEKE BUND	17/3/17		Relieved by 13. E. Batt'n. Royal Sussex Reg'n in the line. & Batt'n went into Brigade reserve. relief complete by 9.50 p.m.	
	17/3/17 to 21/3/17		Batt'n employed on working parties in front line and support and communication trenches. On 21/3/17 Enemy shelled N. end of BUND with heavy artillery. no casualties.	
	21/22/ 3/17		Relieved by 4/5th Royal Highlanders. Relief complete 1.30 a.m. Batt'n marched to Asylum dug-out, entrained to BRANDHOEK, & marched to Montreal Camp.	
MONTREAL CAMP	22/3/17		Batt'n engaged in usual training.	
	24/3/17 to 27/3/17		Batt'n relieved 4/5th Royal Highlanders in right subsection of OBSERVATORY RIDGE sector - Relief complete by 4 P.M. 28 March 1917.	
RUDKIN HO.	28/3/17		Slight artillery activity. Enemy blew up DAVIDSON STREET in two places.	

Army Form C. 2118.

WAR DIARY
or
INTELLIGENCE SUMMARY.
(Erase heading not required.)

Instructions regarding War Diaries and Intelligence Summaries are contained in F. S. Regs., Part II. and the Staff Manual respectively. Title pages will be prepared in manuscript.

Place	Date	Hour	Summary of Events and Information	Remarks and references to Appendices
RUDKIN No. 2	29/3/17		From 2.30 p.m. to 3.45 p.m. the enemy shelled Bn. H.Q. with 8" armour piercing shells, and succeeding in knocking four dug-outs, but only one slight casualty resulted.	I.O.R. wounded
	30/3/17		Enemy shelled STAFFORD STREET with 77 m.ms. at intervals throughout the day.	I.O.R. wounded
	31/3/17		Relieved by 13th R. Sussex Regt. Relief complete by 12.45 a.m. Bn. went into Divisional Reserve with H.Q. at KRUISSTRAAT.	

A.T.R. Robinson
Major
12 R. Sussex Regt.

Confidential

No 14

War Diary
of
2nd Bn R. Sussex Regt.
for
April 1917.

E.W.   H.F.

WAR DIARY
or
INTELLIGENCE SUMMARY.
(Erase heading not required.)

Army Form C. 2118.

Place	Date	Hour	Summary of Events and Information	Remarks and references to Appendices
KRUISSTRAAT	April 1st to April 4th		Battalion provided small working parties from KRUISSTRAAT Companies trained & training in small arms in Ypres	3 O.R. Wounded
OUDKIN HOUS	Apr 5/6/7th		Battalion relieved by 13th R. Fusrs Regt. Relief complete by 1 A.M. Inn lined with occasional shelling of Tuffers Trail (New Jersey) Battalion Headquarters	
	Apr 6/7/7th		Battalion relieved by 9th York Lancs & proceeded to BRANDHOEK by train. Relief complete by 12.15 A.M. arrived in camp at 2 A.M.	1 O.R. Wounded
BRANDHOEK	Apr 7th 8 11th		Battalion provided 280 men & 5 officers for working parties in YPRES all time. Above men were billeted there during the time Battalion was in rest. Also 150 men & 4 officers were buried nightly	
TUILLERIES	April 12th		Battalion relieved 7th K.R.R. in line between TUBERCULUM TUILLERIES. Relief delayed owing to delay in attacking working parties from YPRES not complete until 3 A.M.	2 O.R. Killed 4 O.R. Wounded
	April 13th		Day suffered twice shelled by heavy, no dug out destroyed	
	April 14th		Enemies shelling by heavy Typhon registration	2 OR Wounded
	April 14/15th		Battalion relieved by 11th Northumberland Fusiliers & proceeded to BRANDHOEK by train. Relief complete by 1.15 A.M. arrived in camp 4 A.M.	
BRANDHOEK	April 15th		Cleaning up & preparation for new moving down of platoons	

WAR DIARY or INTELLIGENCE SUMMARY

Army Form C. 2118.

Place	Date	Hour	Summary of Events and Information	Remarks and references to Appendices
IRISH FARM	Apr 17th	2 am	Batt relieves 1/4th Dmt Lancs. Relief complete 2 am first night. Enemy artillery active on front line CAVAN & BILGE trenches firing	
	18th		Shelled with 77m throughout both days. Weather has been rather disposed	
	19th		Enemy machine gun active during night between FINCH LANE & BILGE	
	20th		TR. observed quiet	
	Apr 20th		Enemy shells fell front by and Minenwerfer at 10.30 pm on Whichahn very effective	
			Quiet day & night	
	22nd			
	23rd		Battalion relieved by 13th R.S.R. Relief complete by 11.45 & march to Ouderdom	1. O.R. Wounded
CANAL BANK	Apr 24th		Battalion engaged in naval Gunnery Musketry special attention being given	3.O.R. Wounded
	Apr 28th		to musketry. Lewis Gunners Rifle Grenadiers. Working parties finished at night	
	Apr 28/29th		Battalion relieved by 1/4th Black Watch. Advance to Poperinghe by Coure from there	
			marched to 2 Camp arriving at 2.30 am	
2 Camp	Apr 29/ 30th		Cleaning up & preparing for training & strategical scheme	

O. Magnay Major
2. R.S.R.

Headquarters,
    116th Infantry Brigade.

            Attached please find war diary for month
of May, 1917.

                                    [signature]
                                Lieut. & a/Adjutant,
                                for Officer Commanding
1.6.1917   12th. Bn. R. Suss. R.

Army Form C. 2118.

12 R Sussex Regt

Vol 15

WAR DIARY
or
INTELLIGENCE SUMMARY.
(Erase heading not required.)

Place	Date	Hour	Summary of Events and Information	Remarks and references to Appendices
I Camp	May 30th		Battalion marched to ABEELE entrained there proceeded to ST. OMER	
WIZERNES	May 31st		marched from ST OMER to WIZERNES billets for the night	
			Battalion paraded at 6 a.m. marched into billets at ACQUIN for somewhat funny	
ACQUIN	May 2nd		arrived at 10 a.m.	
	to May 4th		Battalion practiced soft trench exercises attacks keep form &	
	May 4th		junction & attack with new platoon formation	
	May 6th		Battalion took part in Brigade practice for Brigade attack	
	May 7th		Horse trans programme attack Training musketry	
	Aug 8th			
	9th		Brigade attack practise	
	10th		Brigade attack	
WIZERNES	11th		Battalion started return march arrived WIZERNES 11 a.m.	
			remained there for the night	
OEHTEZEELE	15th		Battalion marched to OEHTEZEELE	
WORMHOULT	16th		Battalion marched to WORMHOULT arriving at 10.30 a.m.	
	17th			
	28th		Battalion at rest in WORMHOULT Recreation Spts Football etc.	

WAR DIARY
or
INTELLIGENCE SUMMARY.

Army Form C. 2118.

Place	Date	Hour	Summary of Events and Information	Remarks and references to Appendices
YPRES +	May 28th		2 Companies left WORMHOUDT by Train to YPRES & proceeded with Railway Construction work attached to Canadian R.E. Construction Coy. 1 Coy strides to 11? B.22.	
O Camp.	May 29th		Remainder of Company marched to O Camp	
	May 31st		Battalion relieved 16th R.D. in front line 16/16H 30 c.m. relief HILLTOP relief Complete by 12.30 a.m.	

P. Looy Major.
12th R. Sussex R.

Army Form C. 2118.

WAR DIARY
or
INTELLIGENCE SUMMARY.
(Erase heading not required.)

Original

12 R Sussex
Vol 16.

Place	Date	Hour	Summary of Events and Information	Remarks and references to Appendices
	1917			
HILL TOP R.	June 12 to June 14th		Quiet tour, enemy not active. Occasional shelling of LA BRIQUE Roads shelled heavily at night. Transport reduced owing casualties.	1.O.R. killed 1.O.R wounded 1.O.R gassed
	June 15th		Battalion provided large working parties each night to Inniskillings ARMYTAGE TRENCH	
	June 16		Battalion relieved by 13th R Sussex Regt. returned into Reserve at CANAL BANK. Relief complete by 1. A.m.	7. O.R wounded
CANAL BANK	June 17th to June 19th		Only training carried out on CANAL BANK. Also large working parties provided every night.	1.O.R wounded 4. O.R wounded
HILL TOP R. Rt Sub Sector	June 20th		Battalion relieved 13th R Sussex Regt in front line. Battalion Headquarters LA BRIQUE. Relief complete 1.Am	
	June 21		At about 1.45am whilst working ARMYTAGE TRENCH 2nd Lt F.W. SHEPPARD in charge of wiring party in front line on patrol two scout parties were sent out through wire 2nd Lt SHEPPARD saying it is presumed he was taken prisoner.	11th June 2.O.R killing 5. O.R wounded 1. Officer missing 3.O.R wounded
	June 22nd/23rd		Much trench work carried out during tour. Numerous shelter constructed in FORWARD TRENCH	13 June 3.O.R wounded 14 " 1.O.R " 15 " 1.O.R " 16 " 1.O.R.
O.CAMP	June 24th		Battalion relieved by 17th K.R.R. marched to O.Camp Reserve	16.F. asked

WAR DIARY
or
INTELLIGENCE SUMMARY.
(Erase heading not required.)

Army Form C. 2118.

Place	Date	Hour	Summary of Events and Information	Remarks and references to Appendices
O. CAMP	June 16th } June 17th }		Completed at about 1.45. Two Companies remained at CAMP BANK to provide working parties for June 17th. Remaining 2 Companies arrived at O. CAMP about 4 P.M.	
—	June 17th to June 20th		General training carried out parades attended to borders Rifle Trenches.	
MOULE	June 21st		Battalion marched to POPERINGHE entrained there for WATTEN thence from the latter place by march route to MOULE arriving at 6 P.M.	
—	June 22nd to June 30th		Battalion employed upon Divisional training, stopping routes trenches. New attack formations practised.	

D. May Major
12th Essex Regt.

Original

WAR DIARY
or
INTELLIGENCE SUMMARY.
(Erase heading not required.)

Army Form C. 2118.

12 R Sussex 39
Vol 17

Place	Date	Hour	Summary of Events and Information	Remarks and references to Appendices
	1917			
MOULE	July 12th		Battalion engaged in practice listening patrols attack upon noted trenches	
	July 13th		Arrived attack rehearsal on model trenches under the conditions shown as laid down in practice orders	
	July 16th		Battalion marched to WATTEN entrained thence for HOPOUTRE Siding	
	July 17th		Marched to O. CAMP arriving at 12.30 a.m.	
			Usual training carried on. Inspection of model of enemy trenches by officers & N.C.O's	
O CAMP	July 18th		Usual training and inspection of model carried out. Working parties for carrying ammunition &c to forward dumps supplied every night. One company &c half accompanied to Thought at the CANAL BANK. On the night 23rd/24th 2nd Lt W.F. FISHER was ambushed while patrolling 2nd Lt CARNE the enemy wire. He was wounded and taken prisoner in C.C.S.	5. O.R. killed 11. O.R Wounded 10. O.R. Gassed
	July 24th		severely wounded in CANAL BANK and died afterwards in C.C.S.	
	July 28th		Battalion relieved 6th Bn Lincolns in night entrenches of Hill Top. A coy in Front Line, D on "X" line, B + C coys in CANAL BANK. Relief complete by	1. O.R. killed 2. O.R wounded

WAR DIARY
or
INTELLIGENCE SUMMARY.
(Erase heading not required.)

Army Form C. 2118.

Place	Date	Hour	Summary of Events and Information	Remarks and references to Appendices
HILL TOP	July 29th	12 midnight	Battalion Headquarters in BILGE TRENCH. Enemy confortable quiet. Working & carrying parties supplied by Bn. in CANAL BANK and "X" LINES	1 Officer wounded 1 O.R. wounded
—	July 30th		Hostile shelling slightly increased. At night battalion moved forward to assembly positions in HOPKINS, ARMYTAGE & CAVAN TRENCHES.	
—	July 31st	at 3.50 a.m.	the battalion attacked the enemy front line & support trenches and succeeded in taking & consolidating all objectives with very slight casualties. Estimated casualties to attrition are (60) 2nd Lt. SYMINTON killed & 2nd Lt. J.S. COLLINS wounded.	

W Mooney 21/4
12th Royal Sussex R.

6,000 000 15 7 17
Officer 1
12th Royal Sussex R.

WAR DIARY or INTELLIGENCE SUMMARY

12 R Sussex Vol 18

18.F.
3 sheet

Place	Date	Hour	Summary of Events and Information	Remarks and references to Appendices
	1917			
MOUSE TRAP FARM	Aug 1st		A.1.D Coy held BACK LINE with 13th R.F.F B Coy held BLUE LINE. Enemy heavily shelled BLUE LINE all day making the work of repair at 9 pm this was fairly well accomplished	1st Batt 11 killed 1 officer wounded 12 O.R. killed 3 O.R. missing 102 O.R. wounded
	Aug 2nd		Enemy shelling very heavy on our Battalion relieved by 13th R.F.F not about 3 am relief complete by about 3 am Battalion moved to CANAL BANK. It suffered from the hot parts but arrived until 9 am on the 3rd and	
CANAL BANK	Aug 3rd		Battalion rested in CANAL BANK. Weather very hot.	
X CAMP	Aug 4th	6	Sudden entrained at ASYLUM STATION, YPRES. Proceeded to POPERINGHE marching from there to X CAMP arriving at 2 p.m.	
	Aug 5th		Battalion resumed in cleaning up & refitting	
	Aug 6th			
METERUM	Aug 7th		Battalion proceeded by train from HOPOUTRE to CAESTRE from there to marching to camp in METERUM area	
	Aug 8th Aug 11th		Battalion carried on with cleaning up & refitting. Brigade	
	Aug 12		of the 2nd Army & 10th Corps Commanded	

Army Form C. 2118.

WAR DIARY
or
INTELLIGENCE SUMMARY.
(Erase heading not required.)

Instructions regarding War Diaries and Intelligence Summaries are contained in F. S. Regs., Part II. and the Staff Manual respectively. Title pages will be prepared in manuscript.

Place	Date	Hour	Summary of Events and Information	Remarks and references to Appendices
RIDGEWOOD CAMP	14/8/17		Bn. moved to Ridgwood Camp (Nr. Dickebusch Huts) & relieved the 8th Inns. Regt. (47th Div)	
"	Aug 23		Bn. relieved the 12th Bn Dublin Regt. (3d Div) the Wh R. West Kent Regt. (2 Bn.) on the right sector HOLLEBEKE Sector.	1 J.R. killed 2 O.R. wounded
HOLLEBEKE Aug 24th. BOIS CONFLUENT 1.9 p.m			Bn held line front & rear & intercommunicating trench and relieved by 13th R.I. Rif. R on right 17/B on left, 7th Rif. Bde. Heavy shell coming into the	3 O.R. wounded
			at the BOIS CONFLUENT. B.H.Q. moved back to Ridgwood comp. Without casualty.	
RIDGEWOOD CAMP Aug 24/.			Bn. relieved 13th R. Irish R. in rest R. on the line Relieved by "A" Coy. 17th Royal Sussex Regt 16th Cheshire Regt the 10th Sherwood Foresters Reserve line to	
"	25/.		RIDGEWOOD CAMP.	1 O.R. wounded
RIDGEWOOD CAMP.	26/.		Bde. in charge of Ridgwood comp. 2 Bn goes in support. Relieved the 11th Cheshire Regt in the Right sector (Ellis Bellewke)	1 O.R. wounded
	27/.		ZILLEBEKE SECTOR	

Army Form C. 2118.

WAR DIARY
or
INTELLIGENCE SUMMARY.
(Erase heading not required.)

Instructions regarding War Diaries and Intelligence Summaries are contained in F. S. Regs., Part II. and the Staff Manual respectively. Title pages will be prepared in manuscript.

Place	Date	Hour	Summary of Events and Information	Remarks and references to Appendices
KLEIN ZILLEBEKE	Aug 29/31	—	In support line. 4 days of nightly carrying parties digging. Relieved the 18th R.Innis.F. in the left sub-section KLEIN ZILLEBEKE sector.	2/Lt R wounded

W.M.[?]
Lt/Col my
for O.C. 12th R.Innis.R.

Original

12 R Queen's
1/6/39
Vol 19

19F
2 sheets

WAR DIARY
or
INTELLIGENCE SUMMARY.
(Erase heading not required.)

Army Form C. 2118.

Place	Date	Hour	Summary of Events and Information	Remarks and references to Appendices
RIDGEWOOD	Sept 2nd 1917		Battalion relieved by BEDFORD REGT in KLEIN ZILLEBEKE left trenches marched to RIDGEWOOD Camp	1 O.R. killed 3 O.R. wounded
CHIPPEWA	Sep 4th		Battalion marched to CHIPPEWA Camp at 3 p.m.	
VOORMEZEELE	—	8th	Battalion relieved 1/6 Cheshire Regt in Brigade Reserve	
ZWARTELEEN	—	9th	Battalion marched from VOORMEZEELE to trenches in 129 a. Working parties Cable trenching every night	1 O.R. wounded
RIDGEWOOD	—	11th	Battalion relieved by 17th NOTTS & DERBY — proceeded to RIDGEWOOD Camp Working parties on cable burying at HOLLEBEKE	1 O.R. killed 1 O.R. wounded
ZWARTELEEN	15th & 16th		Relieved the 17th NOTTS & DERBY. Working parties. Heavy shelling.	1 O.R. killed 3 O.R. wounded
WESTOUTRE Kempton Park	18th & 19th		Intervals of heavy shelling Relieved by 17th NOTTS & DERBYS. Captain Aubles O.C. & 5 Officers 1200 men to Ridge Wood. 40 Signallers remain to 117 B[rigade]	1 O.R. killed 20 O.R. wounded
		20th	Attack of 117th B[rigade]. C. Coy & 2 platoons of B. Coy attacked from RAE MSH. 8 S.O.R. wounded. Captain Aubles & 200 men carrying party for SCOTS RIF.	6 O.R. killed 4 O.R. missing
BEGGARS REST		22nd	Relieved 17th NOTTS & DERBYS	

Army Form C. 2118.

WAR DIARY
or
INTELLIGENCE SUMMARY.
(Erase heading not required.)

Place	Date	Hour	Summary of Events and Information	Remarks and references to Appendices
TOWER HAMLETS	Sept 24th	23.24	Bn relieved two companies each of 13th R Suss R & 14th Hants	Officer memoranda 4 8 O.R killed 11 7 O.R wounded 26 O R missing
	25th		Extremely heavy shelling. B Coy sent up to reinforce 11th R of Sussex at Dumbarton Lakes	
	26th		ZERO DAY	
	27th		Bn relieved by 13th Rifle Brigade	
NEAR GERTHEN Sh27 P.23 d.7.	28th		Bn in rest. reorganising cleaning up resting etc	

R Cumbers Capt
D/Adjt R Sust

Original

WAR DIARY
or
INTELLIGENCE SUMMARY.
(Erase heading not required.)

Army Form C. 2118.

12 R Sussex Regt

Vol 20

20 F
3 sheet

Place	Date	Hour	Summary of Events and Information	Remarks and references to Appendices
W. KOKEREELE	28/9/17 to 1/10/17		Battalion training. Route marches carried out on alternate days of eight and ten miles.	
W. Kokereele	2/10/17		Battalion was inspected by the G.O.C. 39th Division. Presentation of Decorations gained on 31/7/17.	
"	3/10/17 to 14/10/17		Training. Gas demonstration by the Divisional Gas Officer. Battalion still training.	
Tower Hamlets	15/10/17		Moved in Busses to SPOIL BANK and marched to relieve the 8th Bn. Lincolns and 8th Batt. Somersets in Tower Hamlets Sector.	
"	16/10/17		Relief complete at 9.55 p.m. Dispositions:— "C" Company Right front, "B" Company Centre front, two Platoons "A" Coy. left front and two Platoons in rear while 1/2 "D" Company in Support. Batln. H.q. at HET PAPPOIE. No Casualties during Relief.	
"	17/18/17		Battalion relieved by 11th Battalion Royal Sussex Regiment. Casualties during two days in front line — 1 Other Rank killed. 9 " " wounded.	
"	17/18/10/17		Moved into Support as follows:— A and B Coys. in HEDGE STREET TUNNELS	

WAR DIARY

INTELLIGENCE SUMMARY.

(Erase heading not required.)

Army Form C. 2118.

Instructions regarding War Diaries and Intelligence Summaries are contained in F.S. Regs., Part II. and the Staff Manual respectively. Title pages will be prepared in manuscript.

Place	Date	Hour	Summary of Events and Information	Remarks and references to Appendices
TOWER HAMLETS	17/10/17		"C" and "D" Coys. in CANADA STREET TUNNELS. Batt. Headquarters in CANADA STREET TUNNELS.	
CANADA STREET	18/10/17		Whole Battalion proceeded to Irmy Cable near MENIN ROAD. RENDEZVOUS. Left Battalion Company Headquarters at J.21.a.0.3. Casualties: KILLED 1 O.R. WOUNDED 18 wounded	
"	19/10/17		Again proceeded to J.21.a.0.3. to Irmy Cable. Casualties: KILLED 1 O.R. WOUNDED 3 O.R.	
"	20/10/17		After completion of Cable Inwying the Battalion proceeded to Camp at N.9.d.7.5 (WITTEBEEK). Training and improving the Camp.	
WITTEBEEK N.9.d.7.5	21/10/17			
"	22/10/17		The Battalion moved in Buses from CONFUSION CORNER to BUS HOUSE and marched from there to a RENDEZVOUS at J.21.a.0.3. to Irmy Cable. From left Battalion headquarters to the front line. Casualties: KILLED 2 O.R. WOUNDED 4 O.R. MISSING 1 O.R.	

WAR DIARY
or
INTELLIGENCE SUMMARY

(Erase heading not required.)

Army Form C. 2118

Instructions regarding War Diaries and Intelligence Summaries are contained in F.S. Regs., Part II. and the Staff Manual respectively. Title Pages will be prepared in manuscript.

Place	Date	Hour	Summary of Events and Information	Remarks and references to Appendices
WIJLEBEEK	23/10/17	2.30 p.m.	The Battalion moved to Camp at DE ZON ANNEXE by march Route via KEMMEL and LOCRE. Camp composed of Irulaul's and tents. Work of building sandbag walls around tents and tents was completed by the Battalion.	
DE ZON ANNEXE	24/6		Training at DE ZON ANNEXE.	
"	28/10/17		Battalion moved on 28th October to camp at MURRUM BIDGEE. Move by march Route commencing at 4-40 p.m.	
MURRUM-BIDGEE.	29/10/17		All in Camp 5-45 p.m. Work of instructing Replica and Model of BERRY COTTS commenced. O.C. Company and his N.C.Os. reconnoitred the objective line held by 17th Cheshires in front of the objective. Training at hours daily.	
"	30/10/17		Construction of Replica and Model of BERRY COTTS nearing completion.	
"	31/10/17		Battalion still training. Construction of Replica and Model of BERRY COTTS completed. Anwall Company (A) practised over the Replica today.	

Lt. Colonel
Comdg. 12th Royal Engineer Regt.
31/10/17

Original

12 R Sussex
Army Form C. 2118.

Vol 21

WAR DIARY
INTELLIGENCE SUMMARY.
(Erase heading not required.)

Place	Date	Hour	Summary of Events and Information	Remarks and references to Appendices
Murrum- idge	1/7		Training for Officers Operators continued	
do do	3/7/7		Battalion entrained for the line relieving 1/1 Herts in support at Tower Hamlets sector	
Tower Hamlets	6/7/17		We relieved the 11 Sussex in the line. "C" Right front. "D" Centre front. "B" Left front. "A" Support	3.O.Rs wounded
Tower Hamlets	14/7		Relieved by the 16th Rifle Brigade. Entrained at Shrapnel Corner for Murrumbidge	
Murrumbidge	15/7		Baths & Cleaning	
do	9/7		Ribbons presented by the R.A.C.	
Tower Hamlets 13/7/17			Relieved to 12 K.R.R. in Tower Hamlets left front line. "C" Right front. "D" Centre front. "B" Support "A" Left front. B Supports	2. Officers wounded 1 Officer died of wounds 8. O.Rs wounded
Tower Hamlets 15/7			Relieved by the 14 Hants. Battalion went into support at Hedge St Tunnels	5.O.R wounded
Hedge St	20/7/7		Battalion went into the line relieving the 14 Hants. "A" Left front "D" Centre front "B" Right front "C" Support.	1.O.R. killed 1.O.R wounded

21 F
Tobin

WAR DIARY or INTELLIGENCE SUMMARY

Army Form C. 2118.

Place	Date	Hour	Summary of Events and Information	Remarks and references to Appendices
Downes Hamlet	22/11/17	6 P.M.	The enemy attempted a raid on our centre post. They came over in 6 parties. Two of them managed to enter our line & were taken prisoner	2 O.Rs wounded
Joucq Hamlet	22/11/17	5.30 P.M.	We observed our line on the right about 200 yards & put werkata on a line with the enemy about 60 yards away.	3 O.Rs killed 3 O.Rs wounded
Tower Hamlet	25/11/17		Battalion relieved by the 14 Hants & went to Hedge Stk.	1 O.R wounded
Hedge St	26/11/17	7.30 P.M.	Battalion entrained at Transport Farm to proceed to Chippewa Camp.	
Chippewa Camp	27/11/17	11.30 A.M.	Battalion entrained at Goldenberghe & Thenne	
Lovrenyck	27/11/17		By march route to Lovrenyck area (Billets for the Battalion)	
Lovrenyck	29/11/17		Battalion moved to Ooringhe and to billets	
do. do	30/11/17		Battalion paraded for working parties near Ypres but the railway was broken & the parties were sent back at Goldenberghe. The railway was broken & the parties returned to Camp and my work.	

O.C. 12/17 2nd Sussex Regt

WAR DIARY
or
INTELLIGENCE SUMMARY.

Army Form C. 2118.

12 R Sussex Regt

Place	Date	Hour	Summary of Events and Information	Remarks and references to Appendices
Poperinghe	1/12/17	6.30 a.m	The Battalion paraded for working parties near YPRES. The following parties were found by Coys. N°1 Party - Half 'D' Coy. at G.3.a.90.10. N°2 - 'A' Coy. at I.1.c.60.00 N°3 - 'B' Coy. at H.5.c. and 11.a. N°4 - 'C' Coy near YPRES on POTIJE Rd. N°5 - Half 'D' Coy at I.7.a.	
"	2/12/17	6.30 a	The same working parties were found.	
"	3/12/17	6.30 a.m	Working parties as before. Half - N°1 Party was cancelled.	
	2 p.m	A Court of Inquiry into 'B' Coy A/c's was held under the Presidency of Capt. Trenchelle.	
"	4/12/17	6.30 a.m	Working parties as before.	
	2 p.m	A Field General Court Martial was held by Maj 172.0.8. Pte. Weatherhog W, under presidency of Major Andrews.	
"	5/12/17	6.30 a.m	Working parties as before.	
"	7/12/17	8.a.m	Battalion paraded and moved to billets in the WINNIZEELE area.	
WINNIZEELE	10/12/17	12.57 p.m	Battalion paraded to move into the LUMBRES Area, marched to GODEWAERSVELDE and entrained for NIELLES-LES-BLEQUIN, whence marched into billets at SENINGHEM and AFFRINGUES.	
SENINGHEM	12/12/17	9 a.m	Training commenced.	

22F
3 what

Army Form C. 2118.

WAR DIARY
or
INTELLIGENCE SUMMARY.
(Erase heading not required.)

Place	Date	Hour	Summary of Events and Information	Remarks and references to Appendices
SENINGHEM	18/12/17	2 p.m	A court of Inquiry was held under the presidency of Capt. Tenbull M.C. to inquire into the method of keeping accounts in the Battalion	
"	19/12/17		Sec Lieut. J.C. Hulley was appointed Asst Adjutant and Intelligence Officer.	
"	20/12/17	8.45am	Battalion was inspected by the Brigadier General commanding.	
"	22/12/17	11.25am	Battalion was inspected by the G.O.C. Division.	
"			Lieut-Col W. Cato-Brown returned from leave and took over the command of the Battalion from Major A.E. Andrews	
"	23/12/17		Training on the small range.	
"	23/12/17	10am	Church Parade.	
"	24/12/17		Training on the small range.	
"	25/12/17	7.15am	Church Parade – Xmas dinners afyn - day spent in rest.	
"	26/12/17	9.30	Short route march – remainder of day rest.	
"	27/12/17		Rest at Baths	
"	28/12/17	9.30am	Batt moved into billets in LOTTING HEM.	
LOTTINGHEM	29/12/17	9.30am	Batt returned to billets in AFFRINGUES & SENINGHEM.	
SENINGHEM	30/12/17	5.30am	Batt move to pasard area. March east via ZERYES - train to LIVE DINGHE.	

Army Form C. 2118.

WAR DIARY
or
INTELLIGENCE SUMMARY.
(Erase heading not required.)

Instructions regarding War Diaries and Intelligence Summaries are contained in F. S. Regs., Part II. and the Staff Manual respectively. Title pages will be prepared in manuscript.

Place	Date	Hour	Summary of Events and Information	Remarks and references to Appendices
HOSPITAL FARM	31/10/17	9am	March route to HOSPITAL FARM CAMP. Arrived about 7pm. Batt'n in Divisional Reserve. Training during the morning. Off'rs recces carried out a reconnaissance of the route to the front line.	

H.E. Allen
Captain
Commanding
12th N. [?] R.

Headquarters
16th Inf Brigade

Herewith War Diary
for month of January 1918

please

M[...]
Capt & Adjt for OC
12 R Sussex R.

31/1/8

WAR DIARY or INTELLIGENCE SUMMARY

Army Form C. 2118.

12 R Sussex

Place	Date	Hour	Summary of Events and Information	Remarks and references to Appendices
	January 1918			
Hospital Farm	1/1/18 and 2/1/18	9 A.m.	Battalion in Divisional Reserve – Training carried out during morning – Reconnaissance of Trenches forward from Brigade H.Q. to Front Line (WESTROOSEBEKE SECTOR) carried out by Officers & NCO's.	
"	3/1/18	9 a.m.	Battalion in Divisional Reserve – Training.	
"	4/1/18	9 a.m.	Battalion carries out musketry Training on Shell Range. Batt. in Brig. Reserve	
"	5/1/18	9 a.m.	Battalion in Brit. Reserve – Training – all behchion preparations. Gas Chamber Bunker reconnaissance of trenches carried out as in 1st & month. F.G.C.M. assembled under Presidency of Captain H.F. ALLEN, The Buffs tried No. 17895 Pte PARKER G. and No. 15794 Pte PORTSMOUTH H. for desertion.	
"	6/1/18	8 am	Battalion at Bath – Siege Camp – Church Parade 2.15 pm.	
"	7/1/18	9 pm	Training – 3.30 pm Battalion moves to IRISH F.M. Camp in relief of 4/5th Black Watch.	
IRISH FM CAMP	8/1/18	5.15 am	Battalion on working parties – Corps Line (STEEN BEEK DEFENCES)	Casualties 2 O Ranks 2 O Ranks
"	9/1/18	5.30 a.m.	ditto	
"	10/1/18	"	ditto	

Army Form C. 2118.

WAR DIARY
or
INTELLIGENCE SUMMARY.
(Erase heading not required.)

Place	Date	Hour	Summary of Events and Information	Remarks and references to Appendices
IRISH FM CAMP	10/1/18	5.30am	Battalion on working parties - Reconnaissance of Front Line	3 O.R. wounded
"	12/1/18	5.30am	Carried out by Officers & Runners. Battalion on working parties	
"	13/1/18	5.30am	ditto. Voluntary Church parade	
"	14/1/18	5.30am	ditto. 1 Officer and NCO's per Company visited	
"			open mode of seeing of Front Line by 11th Corps	
"	15/1/18	3.45pm	Battalion relieved 1st/1st Cambs. in Support Line (STEENBEEK DEFENCES)	
CORPS LINE	16/1/18		Battalion found working parties for Front Line Battalions	
STEENBEEK DEFENCES	17/1/18		ditto	1 O.R. wounded
"	18/1/18		Battalion relieved 13th R. Sussex R. in Right Front - (WESTROOSEBEKE SECTOR)	3 O.R. wounded
			with HQ. at KROMPRINTZ FARM. - Relief complete 9.30pm A.T.B. Coy	
			"B" Left Front Coy respectively. "C" Coy Support. "D" Coy Reserve	
WESTROOSEBEKE (Rt Front)	20/1/18		"D" Coy relieves "A" Coy in right front line. "A" Coy moving into reserve - "C" Coy O.R. wounded	
"			relieves "B" Coy in eft Front Line. "B" Coy moving into support	
"	21/1/18		The Battalion was relieved by the 19th Bn. D.L.I. - Relief complete 8.15 pm	6 O.R. killed 2 O.R. wounded

Army Form C. 2118.

WAR DIARY
or
INTELLIGENCE SUMMARY.
(Erase heading not required.)

Instructions regarding War Diaries and Intelligence Summaries are contained in F.S. Regs., Part II. and the Staff Manual respectively. Title pages will be prepared in manuscript.

Place	Date	Hour	Summary of Events and Information	Remarks and references to Appendices
*	21/1/18	12 midnight	The Battalion on relief marched to WELTJE STN. and entrained to POPERINGHE. Detraining at that RAILHEAD - marched to SCHOOLS CAMP (L.3.d. Sheet 27)	
SCHOOLS CAMP.	22/1/18	—	All in Camp 3 am. Battalion rested -	
POPERINGHE	23/1/18	8am	Battalion at Baths (Township Camp) - General cleaning up. Entire issue 1 new clothing throughout Battalion -	
"	24/1/18	9.00	Battalion Parade - Inspection by C.O. - Training during morning. Inspection of all kits in Battalion by Seconds in Command - Cleaning up kit	
"	25/1/18	9am	General training & inspection of Companies by C.O.	
"	26/1/18	4.15pm	Battalion marched to PROVEN STATION and entrained for MERICOURT. arrived 7am marched to Billets at VAUX-SUR-SOMME - all in	
VAUX-SUR-SOMME	27/1/18	9.30am —	Billets 9.30am 27/1/18 - Battalion rested in billets. Battalion in G.H.Q. Reserve -	
"	28/1/18	9.30am	Training carried out during morning -	
"	29/1/18	9.30am	ditto - 5 Officers carried out reconnaissance of new front - Advance party proceeded to take over	

Army Form C. 2118.

WAR DIARY
or
INTELLIGENCE SUMMARY.
(Erase heading not required.)

"B" 12th Suffolk Regt

No 24

24 F
3 pages

Place	Date	Hour	Summary of Events and Information	Remarks and references to Appendices
HAUT ALLAINES (N. E. PERONNE)	Feby 1918 1st	2 p.m.	The Battalion left billets at HAUT ALLAINES and proceeded by train to HEUDECOURT proceeding from there to relieve 6th K.O.S.B. in the front line – [GAUCHE WOOD sub sector of the GOUZEAUCOURT SECTOR]. "A" Coy on right front company – "B" Coy on left front company – "D" Coy in support and "C" Coy in Reserve – Relief Completed at 8.30 p.m.	
GAUCHE-WOOD SUB SECTOR	4th		The Battalion were relieved in the front line by the 13th R. Sco R. and moved to Billets as Battalion in Brigade Reserve at HEUDECOURT. "C" "D" Companies furnished working parties in the front line after relief – Allied billets at 1.50 a.m. 5th Feb. Casualties during three days tour in line – 1 O.R. accidently killed	
HEUDECOURT	5th		The Battalion remained in billets in brigade Reserve. 2 Companies provided working parties during the night for work on QUENTIN REDOUBT and front line	
"	6th	8 a.m.	Battalion assisted Baths. 3 Companies provided working parties to front line tr.	
"	7th	10 a.m.	The Divl. Gen'l inspected candidates for Infantry 4 Bn.	
"	8th	7.30 a.m.	Draft of 1 off + 51 oth joined at 7th Suff R. Knives + R/ + proceeded by train to join bn.	

WAR DIARY or INTELLIGENCE SUMMARY.

Army Form C. 2118.

Place	Date	Hour	Summary of Events and Information	Remarks and references to Appendices
Hurtvent	8th	4.30p	Draft of 60/ft & 122 ott arrived to join the 11th Nrfk Regt	
			Rfft went with Gande arms seats	
		5.4p	Draft of 6 off + 134 mn arrived to join the 13th Royal Sussex Rgt	
			Undertoken the Gande wood section	
	10th	6.30am	Draft of 1 off. 101 ott proceeded to join 9th Batt Royal Sussex Rgt.	
	12th	7.30am	Draft of 1 off. 51 ott proceeded to join 8th Batt R. Sussex Rgt	
	14th	9a	Batt H.Q. & Surplus joined Aaworth Reinforcement Camp at Haut Allaines.	
			Transport attached to 118 Inf Bde.	
Haut Allains	16th	9a	B. HQ. & surplus moved to Sorel le Grand	
			Transport bombed 19 horses killed & 8 wounded	
Sorel	17th	8a	HQ's & surplus moved to Hamel & found worthy	
			latin for R.E's at Rocroi station.	
Hamel	18th/19		Working parties at Rocroi —	
	20		Moved to Haut Allains & joined 17th Entrenching Batt	

Army Form C. 2118.

WAR DIARY
or
INTELLIGENCE SUMMARY.
(Erase heading not required.)

Place	Date	Hour	Summary of Events and Information	Remarks and references to Appendices
Hautallain	22		16 Signallers to O.R. transferred to 17th Entrenching Batt.	
	23rd		Two O.R. transferred to 17th Entrenching Batt.	
	28th		Twelve Warrant Officers, N.C.Os. succeeded to Depôt Eight Capt Carnie M.C. Adjutant 1 L. & D. Mr. Secretts and 1 O.R.	
	28th		transferred to 17th Entrenching Battalion	

1st March 1918 –

W. Crole-Brown
Lt. Col.
Comdg 10th M Surrey Regt

www.ingramcontent.com/pod-product-compliance
Lightning Source LLC
Chambersburg PA
CBHW081553160426
43191CB00011B/1920